Algebra

Basic algebra explained

Studymates

British History 1870-1918: The Emergence of a Nation
Warfare 1792-1918: How War became Global
Hitler and Nazi Germany: The Seduction of a Nation (3rd edn)
The English Reformation: The Effect on a Nation
European History 1870-1918: The Rise of Nationalism
Lenin, Stalin and Communist Russia: The Myth and reality
    of Communism
Genetics: The Science of genetics revealed (2nd edn)
Organic Chemistry: how organic chemistry works (2nd edn)
Chemistry: As. Chemistry Explained
Chemistry: Chemistry Calculations Explained
The New Science Teacher's Handbook
Mathematics for adults: Basic Mathematics Explained
Calculus: how calculus works
Understanding Forces: How forces work
Algebra: Basic algebra explained
Plant Physiology: The Structure of plants explained
Poems to Live By
Shakespeare: The Barriers Removed
Chaucer: Approaching the Canterbury Tales
Poetry: The Secret Gems of Poetry Revealed
Better English: Handle everyday situations with confidence
Better French: become fluent in everyday speech
Better German: become fluent in everyday speech
Better Spanish: become fluent in everyday speech
Social Anthropology: the science of people
Statistics for Social Science: data handling explained
Study Skills: maximise your time to pass exams
Practical Drama and Theatre Arts: practical theatre
    skills explained
The War Poets 1914-18: the secrets of poems from the Great War
The Academic Essay: how to plan, draft, write and revise
Your Master's Thesis: how to plan, draft, write and revise
Your PhD Thesis: how to plan, draft, revise and edit your thesis

Many other titles in preparation

Helping You to Achieve

Algebra

Basic algebra explained

Graham Lawler

MA, Adv Dip Educ, Cert Ed, Cert Online Ed

'If a man's wit be wandering, let him study the Mathematics'
Francis Bacon *Essays* (1625)

For young Alex Morrison, for whom I am proud to be
Grandpa Taid.

ISBN 1-84285-068-7

First published in 2005 by Studymates Limited.
PO Box 2, Bishops Lydeard, Somerset TA4 3YE, United Kingdom.

www.studymates.co.uk

Typeset by Ferdinand Pageworks
Printed and bound in the United Kingdom by The Baskerville Press Ltd.

Contents

Author Preface

There are a number of reasons why the study of algebra is important. Her are just three of them.

Algebra is the study of patterns and sequences. By understanding underlying patterns and sequences we can make predictions and it is this ability to predict that means we have power, real power.

Adults often say, 'I have never used algebra in my life after leaving school'. Whilst it is probably true that they have never used algebra in the sense of manipulating equations, what they most certainly have done is to have used algebraic thinking techniques.

We will discuss in C1.

The second reason why algebra is important is that in many examinations it is used as the discriminator question. This means that in examinations, students who have demonstrated their ability to use algebra will be graded higher than those who have not. I have seen examination papers where two students both gained $62^1/_2$%, one was given a higher grade than the other. The one with the higher grade had shown he could solve equations whilst the lower grade student could not. The algebra was used as a mechanism to distinguish between their performances.

My author and broadcasting colleague John Florance who quotes Dr Jonathon Miller told me the third reason. He told me that Miller paused partway through a lecture and in delight exclaimed 'Isn't it great just to know that …'. This is true about the algebra. As a mathematics educator I want people to delight in the knowledge of the mathematics because it is a subject worthy of study in its own right, and not simply as some utilitarian handmaiden to other areas of study and this is something that we must never lose.

This book is an introduction to algebra. It explains many of the basic skills that you need. It simply is impossible to cover everything in one text but I hope you will use it and learn from it. There are no limits on what you can learn, unless you yourself put them there. As I have said before, elsewhere, believe in yourself, you do have talent.

In writing this book I am indebted to a number of people, particularly my editor Tony Clappison and typesetter Mary Ferdinand who between them turned my notes into a book, my colleague Susanne McDadd from Publishing Services, my designer Matt Knight of Knight Design and the ever-helpful comments from Jane Furlong of Soar Valley College, Leicester. But most of all my thanks go to Judith Lawler, my wife, for having the good grace to put up with the demands a writer makes on family life. I am dedicating this book to Alex Morrison who is too young to understand any of it at the moment, but who will one day pick it up and read these words and understand something of the joy he has brought to the family.

Graham Lawler
graham.lawler@studymates.co.uk

Learning and doing Mathematics

There is an old maxim in mathematics education that says ' the only way to learn mathematics is to do mathematics'. This is very true. It really is important to have a go at the questions in this book and to note down your responses in your journal. This will provide you with an ongoing record of your mathematical development.

But are there are short cuts?

Well yes and no. It depends on what you mean by shortcuts. There are ways of working that mean you will work smarter. By smarter we mean you will be more effective.

The first is time management.

- Whenever you study, split your hour up into 3 fifteen-minute study sessions with three five minute breaks. Don't save all the breaks up to the end it simply will not work that way. This is because there is a law in psychology called the law of primacy and recency. This means that by building in breaks in this way we have described you are learning more effectively.

- Whenever you set out to learn, be aware of what it is you are studying. You must have the 'big picture' before you can put the smaller components together.

- At the end of every study session review what you have done.

- Use the review rules. (see below)

The second is to learn mind mapping.

- Mind mapping is an information retrieval system created by British psychologist Tony Buzan.

- Mind mapping is a way of learning that works with the mind. It speeds up your learning and means that you can recall far more information than you originally thought possible. We highly recommend *The Mind Map Book* (BBC Books)

The third is to review your work.

- There are review rules. They are 10 minutes, 1 day, 3 days, 1 week, 3 weeks, 1 month, 3 months, 1 year, 3 years. Whenever you study a new piece of work, make a mindmap. Then using your diary plan in dates when you need to review the mindmap. So simply read over it, tracing out the branches of the mindmap with your finger. And say every piece of information out loud. This gives you multiple sensory inputs into the brain and impacts on your learning.

- Then draw the mindmap from memory on to scrap paper. Make dates in your diary to repeat this practice. By the time you get to 3 years, you should be an expert.

Just remember you can learn, you can improve your performance. Anyone who studies a subject for about 3000 hours can become competent in that area. Anyone who studies a subject for about 10 000 hours can become an expert in that area.

That person really could be you!

What is the Point of Algebra?

One-minute overview

The purpose of algebra is a mystery to many students and parents. The fact is that it is seen as irrelevant, as a useless mind numbing exercise and as something that 'egg heads' work through, just for the sake of it. Nothing could be further from the truth.

In this chapter, we will look at:
- why algebra was invented;
- who invented algebra;
- where do we use algebra in real life;
- how to think algebraically.

Life in the twenty-first century

There are some things in life that we can be fairly comfortable with predicting. One of these is that life in the twenty-first century is going to be one of rapid change. Research has shown that the adult of the future will have to be able to respond quickly to changing circumstances. There is no such thing as a job for life. Older people may remember a time in the last century when young people could expect to join an organisation and stay there for the whole of their career.

These days we are more likely to have a situation where people have two or three careers in their lifetime. To be successful, the citizens of the future need to have a good basic education but also need to be able to think analytically. They need to be able to:

- solve problems;

- write solutions to problems in a general form;

- communicate their ideas to other people.

So why is algebra important?

Algebra develops your thinking ability. It also gives you quite sophisticated thinking tools that you can use in industry – *and* despite what is popularly thought, the algebra you learn in class is more important than ever before. Can you think of just one common use for algebra? Most businesses use spreadsheets in some way or other – spreadsheet formulae are just algebraic statements that do the calculations for you, but if the formulae are wrong, you get the wrong answer.

So there is an even greater need to understand algebra than ever before. You really do ignore it at your peril. Algebra can literally help your career progression. The spreadsheet shown here is a very simple one for a simple set of calculations. The second picture shows the spreadsheet with the formulae on show – look at all the algebra in column D.

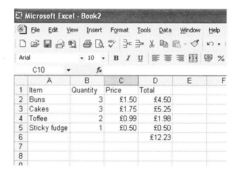

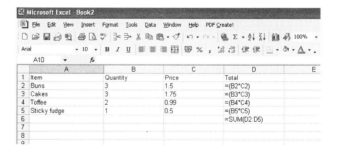

Screenshots reprinted by permission of the Microsoft Corporation

These are very simple formulae but it does give you an example of what is involved.

So why do we need algebra?

The simple answer is that algebra gives us general rules. Look at this example to see what we mean.

Start	1	2	3	4
End	5	7	9	11

What is done to the start number to get the end number? In each case we manipulate the start number with two operations. The first is to multiply by 2 and the second is to add 3. So in each case, we have

start number $\times$ 2 + 3 = end number.

This is a *general* rule that frees up our thinking. Now we can work out the end number for any start value. Say we start with 10 – multiply this by 2, then add 3, and the end number should be 23.

This is a very basic example of how algebra works. The point we want you to understand is that by using algebra, you can understand patterns and sequences that occur in real life.

When you understand these patterns and sequences, you can make predictions about what is going to happen in the future. This is often referred to as 'mathmagic'. In fact it is not magic at all – it is the skill of understanding patterns and thereby being able to predict what will happen. This is what gives us real power. It is this ability to make these predictions that is the most exciting aspect of algebra, this is what fires most mathematicians.

The purpose of this book is to make sure you have some basic skills that will support your learning. But there is one caveat that you must agree to. There is only one way to *learn* mathematics, and that is to *do* mathematics. You do need to sit down and have a go at the problems that are in this book. You need to grapple with the contexts and, as you do, you will join all those who have ever learned mathematics. It is an essential part of the journey to make errors and to learn from them.

So where did algebra come from?

Algebra is a word that is derived from an early Arabic mathematician called Al-Khwarizimi. He most certainly was a genius of his time. We actually know very little about his life but we do know that his family came from Khorezm, at that time in Persia. He worked in the House of Wisdom in Baghdad in present day Iraq. This was a centre for scientific research and teaching. It was his book on algebra that both gave name to the area of study and moved the subject forward. He stated at the time that he wanted to support scholars in the solution of complex problems that occurred at that time. This is still the case today. Algebra allows us to see general patterns and to use this knowledge to solve problems. Al-Khwarizimi went further than this – he wanted to understand and develop the more theoretical aspects of algebra, the science of equations.

By determining rules, we can follow them and calculate answers to matters that previously we could not solve.

For example, you often see calculations like this in children's mathematics textbooks. The diagram shows a playground that measures 10 m by 5 m. Find the area of the playground.

10m

5m

We can use a simple piece of algebra to show the relationship between length and area.

$$\text{area} = \text{width} \times \text{height}$$
$$A = w \times h$$
$$= 10 \times 5$$
$$= 50\,\text{m}^2.$$

A simple example but one which shows an important principle and hints at the power of equations.

Fear and algebra

Many students develop a fear of algebra because they find it hard. If you do get stuck, think about what you would do if you were dealing with numbers instead of letters. Algebra is based on the same set of rules, so you can use the same methods to solve problems. It will help you to understand the work. This is called specialising.

However, in this chapter we want to concentrate on getting you *ready* to learn. That means examining your own motivations and challenging your own perceptions. In other words, it means a taking long hard think about yourself. What is it that you cope well with and what is it that frightens you? Think about this for a moment.

Personal journal

We suggest that you consider writing a 'personal journal' to record your thoughts and fears – this is a great way of challenging them and taking control of your life, rather than letting events control you.

Keep the journal private – it is for you, not for anyone else. It is your private world where you can channel your thoughts and develop the confidence that you deserve.

Feeling the fear

Fear comes from within. It is how you *respond* to events that affect you, rather than the events themselves. Think about this for a moment. Everyone has downsides in life, so why is it that some people give up and others move on with a smile on their face?

Quite simply it is because they can control how they respond. They are in charge of their emotions and not servant to them. When it comes to mathematics, many people take fright. Certainly in the western world it can be seen as a badge of pride to publicly declare, 'I am no good at maths'. Yet the same people wouldn't dream of admitting that they cannot spell or write.

It is as if they see themselves as unsullied by the modern era and more in keeping with a nineteenth century aristocrat who centres life on pleasure. Frankly this is not a sustainable attitude in the twenty-first century. Parents, and indeed teachers, are often heard to say to children, 'Well I could never do maths when I was your age'. This is a dreadful thing to say to a child – in reality the adult is telling the child that it is possible to live in today's society without this level of knowledge, yet how many would say this to a child regarding their spelling? Yes it is meant in sympathy but actually it is sending the wrong message. Children need to be able to spell and they need to be numerate. In the same way, adults need to be numerate and to be able to use algebra. Most people do not take fright when they see sentences in, say, French or German and yet become panic stricken when they see a few symbols of algebra on a page. Algebra is a language in the same way that French or German are languages.

In her excellent book *Feel the Fear and Do It Anyway* (Rider, 1997), Susan Jeffers gives good advice on overcoming feelings of insecurity. She writes about that nagging little voice inside all our heads that she calls 'the chatterbox', which is in fact the voice of our lower self. To overcome this one of the most powerful tools to use is the affirmation.

What is an affirmation?

An affirmation is a positive statement that you can say to yourself. This has the effect of lifting you mentally. Think of your brain as a muscle. In the same way that you have to exercise your body, you also need to exercise your brain – affirmations are a great way of doing this.

Just pause for a moment, sit back and …

$$b—r—e—a—t—h—e$$

Now make an affirmation. One of the people in the *Mr Educator* office (www.mreducator.com) said that her affirmation is

'I am loved and I am loving. I am strong and I am powerful.' Who could fail to be inspired with words like these? I hope you find them as uplifting as we do here in the office. See how powerful you become by simply affirming your belief.

The other side of this coin is to label yourself as a failure. We saw a young man in Taunton literally labelling himself negatively. He was walking through the town wearing a shirt with the word 'loser' printed across the front, for all of the world to see. You become what you believe. Believe you are powerful and successful and then you will become powerful and successful. If you believe you are a failure then don't be surprised if that is what you become.

Changing your physiology

Think about how you sit or stand or walk. Your body needs oxygen to work effectively but if your chest cavity is depressed you simply cannot get the oxygen into your lungs – so how can you expect your body and your brain to work well?

In the same way, for peak performance you need to consider your diet. To become a champion in any field you need to provide your body and brain with the right food. Over a third of Americans are obese. That means more than 30% of their body mass is made up of fat. Here in the UK we are not far behind. Thomas Mofat , a seventeenth century American medic said, 'We are digging our graves with our teeth'.

How true this is today. To change the way you feel – to be empowered, to feel great – you need the right exercise and the right food.

What about shortcuts?

There are some shortcuts to improving how you feel. One is to stand up straight and let the tensions in you simply 'wash away'. Changing your physiology changes the way you breathe and this can help you to feel better.

So, why are you reading all of this in a book on algebra?

Quite simply, you cannot perform well mentally if you cannot perform well physically. Doing algebra, and indeed mathematics, is like being a mental tradesman. In the same way that a plumber will select the right tool for the right job from a toolbox, so a mathematician needs to make the same decisions concerning mathematics tools.

In the same way that a plumber may use a wrench, so a mathematician may choose to use a mental tool to solve a problem – but not if they are mentally and physically unfit.

Why do we need algebra?

We have already asked this question, and to some extent answered it, but here we want to take you into this a little deeper.

Robert Reich was a member of President Clinton's US administration and wrote a very influential book called *The Work of Nations*. In this he explains how society has changed since the middle to late 1970s.

Different types of jobs

Reich explains how workers can be put into one of three groups – in-person providers, routine producers and symbolic analysts.

- *In-person providers* are people who do jobs that cannot currently be done by machines. For example the office cleaner or the person in the fast-food outlet who serves you fries are in-person providers. Similarly teachers are in this group.

- *Routine producers* are people who do unskilled or semi-skilled routine work, perhaps in a factory.

  People in both of these groups have seen a fall in their incomes in real terms.

- *Symbolic analysts* are people who use symbols, manipulate them and solve problems symbolically in a way that can then be applied back to the real world to solve problems. A good example is the person who works out the minimum distance route for a delivery van. Symbolic analysts are not the same as graduates. You can be a symbolic analyst if you solve problems at any level in industry. Think of this as a 'troubleshooter' type of job. This is exactly the type of job in which there is a shortage of qualified men and women – and this is where algebra comes into its own and where algebra and this book can help give you a major advantage.

Algebra helps you to learn how to think systematically. It enables you to deal with changes in a system and to define rules that are both simple and elegant.

The elegant equation?

Can an equation really be elegant? Well, yes it can. Look at Einstein's work on relativity. He summarised his work with the elegant and beautiful equation

$$E = mc^2$$

Here Einstein tells us that

energy = mass × the speed of light squared.

Think about the beauty of this equation – Einstein found that a law of the Universe could be described in such a straightforward manner. This is the power of algebra.

Thinking algebraically

There is a style of thinking that mathematicians call algebraic or mathematical thinking. This style, or approach, to thinking is an important life skill. Many people say that they never use algebra after they leave school. Whilst this is undoubtedly true in terms of manipulating symbols, it is unlikely that they have *never* used mathematical thinking.

Here is a simple example. Imagine putting up shelves in your home. Say you need 4 screws for each shelf, what will the total number of screws needed? Think about this for a moment.

The number of screws will be 4 times the number of shelves.

This is a simple example of a generalisation.

Are there other areas in life that use algebra?

There most certainly are – particularly in business. There are established rules, written as equations, that can be applied to solve problems. There are equations that calculate how fast something is travelling. There are equations that calculate the minimum pathway through a production process – this makes it possible to calculate the shortest route through a production process, thereby getting the raw materials into the final form in the shortest possible time. This saves time, and therefore money, and gets the product to market as soon as possible.

Tutorial

Progress questions

Using your journal, answer these questions.

1 What controls you? Are you really controlled by symbols on a page?

2 What would it mean to you if you could improve your education?

3 Would this lead to better job prospects?

Discussion points

When someone is reading material on a subject of which they have little experience, it is easy to fall into reading in a very passive manner.

Practical assignment

1 Where will you in three years time?

2 What type of job will you be doing?

3 Will you be living somewhere else?

Study tips

Learn to 'mind map'. Mind mapping was invented by Tony Buzan and it is an extraordinary way of learning and recording information. Read Tony's book *The Mind Map* (BBC books).

Number Patterns and Sequences

Algebra is all about patterns and sequences – it is about looking for the general from the particular.

In this chapter, you will learn:
- how to describe square numbers, cube numbers and triangle numbers;
- how to describe a sequence;
- how to make simple generalisations.

Square numbers

Some numbers make a pattern that can be shown as a geometric pattern. Look at this sequence.

☆	☆ ☆ ☆ ☆	☆ ☆ ☆ ☆ ☆ ☆ ☆ ☆ ☆
1	**4**	**9**

Can you see the pattern? Look at what you can see – what have the patterns got in common?

Don't worry if you can't see the connection yet – frankly, most people will not. This is an important part of learning mathematics.

The next number is 16. Here it is

☆ ☆ ☆ ☆
☆ ☆ ☆ ☆
☆ ☆ ☆ ☆
☆ ☆ ☆ ☆

16

Can you see the pattern yet? Look at the length and width of the rectangles, what do you notice? Can you predict the next number?

The next number in the sequence is 25 – but why? Look at the arrangement of the dots. You should see that the pattern of the dots is a square, so these numbers are called *square numbers*.

Look again at the squares.

1 is a square number because it is 1×1
4 is 2×2
9 is 3×3
16 is 4×4
25 is 5×5
and so on

Now you can see what these numbers have in common. They follow the pattern that they have the same number of dots in the rows as they have in the columns (well they are squares, so that is what you would expect).

Can you predict what the next number will be? This is the true power of the mathematics, the ability to predict and to be right.

It will be useful to know and be able to recall all the square numbers at least up to 15×15. As well as this you need to know and be able to recall 20×20 and 25×25.

Study tip	Make a chart of all of these square numbers and put it on your wall. This will be a visual stimulus to remind you of what these numbers mean.

The sequence with this formula

$$n^{\text{th}} \text{ term} = n^2$$

is the sequence of square numbers. The first four terms are

1, 4, 9 and 16. The 10th term is 100 (10 × 10) and the 20th term is 400 (20 × 20).

Look again at the sequence 1, 4, 9, 16. None of the rules 'add 3', 'add 5' or 'add 7' work here because the number to add on changes. The rule is first add 3, then add 5, then add 7. So we need to add 9 to get the next term

16 + 9 = 25.

You can see this is correct because we know the next term is 5 × 5.

Square roots

There is a Donald Duck video on mathematics that actually shows cartoon trees with square roots (*Donald in Mathmagic Land*, Disney). This is a great visual image and worth keeping in mind. But what exactly is the square root of a number?

The easiest way to think of this is to consider the square numbers we talked about when we were explaining square numbers. Remember the square number 9 was generated by 3 × 3. So 3 is the square root of 9, because 3 × 3 = 9. In the same way, 5 is the square root of 25 because 5 × 5 = 25. And 10 is the square root of 100 for the same reason.

The square root symbol

$\sqrt{}$ is the symbol for the square root of a number. So the square root of 9 is written as $\sqrt{9}$ and mathematically we write

$$\sqrt{9} = 3.$$

Exercise 2.1

Write down the square roots of all the square numbers up to 225.

Cube numbers

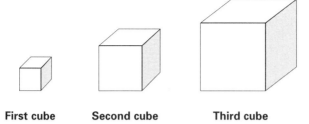

First cube   **Second cube**   **Third cube**

To work out the volume multiply the length by the width by the height. Look at the first cube.

$$\text{volume} = l \times w \times h$$
$$V = 1 \times 1 \times 1$$
$$= 1.$$

So the first cube number is 1.

Now do the same with the second cube.

$$V = 2 \times 2 \times 2$$
$$= 8.$$

> Don't confuse 2^3 with 2 x 3 = 6, this operation is
> 2 x 2 = 4
> then
> 4 x 2 = 8

This means the second cube number in the sequence is 8.

Now do the same with the third cube.

$$V = 3 \times 3 \times 3$$
$$= 27.$$

> 3 x 3 = 9,
> then
> 9 x 3 = 27

Now we do the same with the next number in the sequence. Here we have not drawn a cube, but if it makes things easier then draw your own cube and calculate the fourth cube number. Here is the calculation.

$$V = 4 \times 4 \times 4$$
$$= 64.$$

> 4 x 4 = 16,
> then
> 16 x 4 = 64

So this means that the first four cube numbers are 1, 8, 27 and 64. What are the next three cube numbers? Have a go at this now.

Look at this formula, n^3. Put 1 into the formula – what do you get?

You should have found that you get 1. Let's look at this more closely using the idea of function machines.

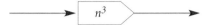

Here if we put 1 into the function machine, we operate n^3 on it. But what does 'operating n^3' mean?

n^3 means $n \times n \times n$.

So when we enter 1 into this function machine it operates as $1 \times 1 \times 1$ so we get 1 out.

What would we get if we put 2 into this function machine? … don't worry we'll wait.

You should have found you get 8 out. Think about it – if we put 2 into the function machine we are operating $2 \times 2 \times 2$. So $2 \times 2 = 4$, then $4 \times 2 = 8$.

So the first two numbers in this sequence are 1 and 8. These are the first two numbers in the sequence of *cube numbers*.

Exercise 2.2
Write down the first five cube numbers. We have the first two, namely 1 and 8. Remember the pattern

$1 \times 1 \times 1 = 1$
$2 \times 2 \times 2 = 8.$

So what are the next three? Please do this before you go any further.

It really is important that you go through the thinking process because that is the power of mathematics. It empowers you to think and to stay ahead of the crowd –but only if you engage with the learning material.

The thinking process here is:

Try this now, look back at what you have done and convince yourself that you are right. Then convince another person.

Triangular numbers

What are the next three numbers in the sequence? Look at the pattern again. It starts with 1, then it is 1 + 2, then 1 + 2 + 3, then 1 + 2 + 3 + 4. The next number will be the answer to 1 + 2 + 3 + 4 + 5, which is …?

Work out the rest of the sequence for the first ten triangular numbers.

What is a sequence?

A sequence is a set of numbers that are connected in some way. For example, a very simple sequence is 3, 6, 9, 12. Obviously this is the three-times table, otherwise known as the multiples of three. Most people recognise this sequence and can simply add the next three numbers: 15, 18, 21.

Example 1
Write down the next six numbers in this sequence.

1, 4, 9, 16, 25, – , – , – , – , – , – .

Explain how the sequence is made. Do this before you read any further.

We have met this sequence before – it is very important and you need to remember it. It is called the sequence of square numbers. Another way of writing the sequence is

$1 \times 2, 2 \times 2, 3 \times 3, 4 \times 4, 5 \times 5, \ldots$

Now it is easy to see how the sequence actually generates. In terms of shape,

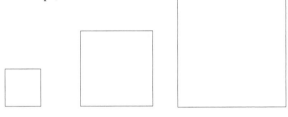

| First square | Second square | Third square |

Again, convince yourself and then convince another person.

We have mentioned square numbers previously, have a look at the earlier mention in this chapter. It is important that you feel comfortable with this sequence.

Example 2

Can you see how this sequence is building up?

$1, 1, 2, 3, 5, 8, -, -, -, \ldots$

This is a very famous sequence. It was discovered by a medieval Italian mathematician called Fibonacci – it is called the 'Fibonacci sequence'. The pattern builds up by adding together the previous two numbers.

- It starts at 1.

- There is nothing in front of the first 1, so $0 + 1 = 1$ and we generate the second 1.

- $1 + 1 = 2$ so we generate the 2.

- In the same way, $1 + 2 = 3, 2 + 3 = 5, 3 + 5 = 8$, and so on.

What is the next number in the Fibonacci sequence?

Generalising

Generalisations are simple rules that connect two sets of numbers. We usually write these rules in the language of algebra. To get you in the mood let's play a game – it is the start–end game that we met briefly in Chapter 1.

Example 1

Start	1	2	3	4	5
End	2	4	6	8	10

This is a very simple example to get you started. What do you do to the start numbers to get to the end numbers? Obviously you need to multiply by 2, or to double them.

So, the rule for this game is

start number $\times$ 2 = end number

This can be written this algebraically

$s \times 2 = e$, or more correctly, $2s = e$.

This reads as 2 multiplied by the start number (s) equals the end number (e).

We have made a simple generalisation here – we have found a rule that applies to every start number in this set of numbers and takes us to every end number.

Example 2

Start	1	2	3	4	5	6
End	3	6	9	12	15	18

What is the rule? OK you have probably found it already, but just in case, we want to talk you through a technique useful for finding rules like this.

Look at the end numbers first – here they are again.

3

6

9

12

15

18

Now we look for what are called the *first differences*. In other words we are looking for what jumps they go up in. Look at this:

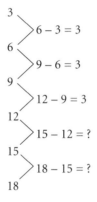

3

$6 - 3 = 3$

6

$9 - 6 = 3$

9

$12 - 9 = 3$

12

$15 - 12 = ?$

15

$18 - 15 = ?$

18

You should have noticed that they are all going up in threes. What does this tell you? What do you know that goes up in a steady step of 3? The answer must be the three-times table.

So first differences can be used to give us an early clue about a sequence and its pattern. The next thing to do is to multiply the start number by the first difference and see if this gives the end number? Does it work for every start number and take you to every end number?

If the answer is yes, then you have found the rule that links the start and end numbers. *But what if it doesn't?*

Example 3

Start	1	2	3	4	5	6
End	5	8	11	14	17	20

First, work out the first differences.

$8 - 5 = 3$
$11 - 8 = 3$
$14 - 11 = 3$
...

You will agree that the first differences are 3. This gives a clue as to what to multiply the start numbers by. Now, $1 \times 3 = 3$, but the end number is 5 – what is going on?

In Example 2 in this section we had the function machine

In this example we have something slightly different

In other words there are two operations taking place here. The first we have identified with the first differences, we now need a second operation. Think about what this operation might be for a moment.

The question is, after we have multiplied the start number by 3, we get an interim number. What do we do with that interim number to get the end number? Think about this now and make an entry in your journal – this is an important part of your mathematical thinking development.

> **Study tip** Writing something down makes it real for your brain. It really is worth the effort to write it down, it makes your learning more effective.

Have you worked it out? Clearly it must be that you add 2.
So the complete operation is

We can write that algebraically as $3s + 2 = e$.

Exercise 2.3
Work out the rule for each of the sequences below. Write
your answers as algebraic equations.

1

Start	2	3	4	5	
End	10	15	20	25	

2

Start	1	2	3	4	5
End	4	7	10	13	16

3

Start	10	11	12	13	14	15
End	101	111	121	131	141	151

4

Start	9	10	11	12	14
End	21	23	25	27	31

5

Start	16	17	18	19	20
End	49	52	55	58	61

Tutorial

Progress questions

1 Write down the first four square numbers.

2 Calculate:

   a $\sqrt{100}$ **b** $\sqrt{144}$ **c** $\sqrt{400}$

3 What are the first four cube numbers?

4 What is the next square number after 144?

Discussion points

The more you play with numbers, the easier they become to manipulate.

How true is this for you? Make a comment in your journal.

Practical assignment

Develop a start–end game as a party game for your friends. Try to develop the algebraic thinking of your friends.

3 The Power of the Index

One-minute overview

In order to be a successful cook or joiner, you have to have mastery of your tools. A cook who doesn't understand what a cake tin is for, or how to grease it, will not bake good cakes. A joiner who doesn't know how to put a bit in a drill will not have a long career in joinery. So the little skills are important. As a mathematician you need to understand certain skills that you will use later.

In this chapter we will look at:
- the highest common factor of two or more numbers;
- the lowest common multiple of two or more numbers;
- how to write numbers as powers;
- how to multiply and divide powers.

Directed numbers and indices

Numbers are either positive or negative. Think about what happens to a bank account if you become overdrawn. If you have £3 in an account and take out £5, you have an overdraft of £2. In other words you owe the bank £2. Mathematically, this can be written this as −£2. So your account is −£2. So −2 is obviously 2 less than zero.

Another way to think of numbers is on a temperature scale. Clearly, on a frosty winter morning when you see someone scraping ice off a car the temperature is less than zero. To be able to signify what the temperature is we need to use the negative sign. So a temperature lower than zero has a minus sign in front of it.

How do we think of negative numbers?

When you are studying mathematics, a good way forward is to create a mental model. By this we mean something that you can recall at will, to work things out in your head.

A good way of thinking about negative numbers is to imagine a block of flats or apartments. This is only a mental model so we can be a bit silly – this block goes up through the clouds as far as the eye can see. In addition the block carries on down underground.

The ground level floor is named 'zero'. This means that the first floor above ground level is +1, the second is +2 and so on. But what do we call the first floor *below* ground level? We cannot call it +1 because this refers to the first floor *above* ground level. So the first floor below ground level has to be –1. The second floor below is therefore –2 and the third floor is –3 and so on. Think of this as a diagram.

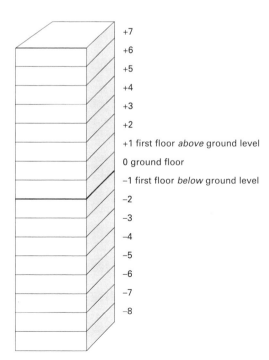

+7
+6
+5
+4
+3
+2
+1 first floor *above* ground level
0 ground floor
–1 first floor *below* ground level
–2
–3
–4
–5
–6
–7
–8

This mental model will be useful when working with directed (positive and negative) numbers. When you are adding you are going up the block – when you are subtracting you are going down the block.

So if you were on the first floor above ground level, at +1, and you then went down 4 floors where would you be? Mathematically this can be written

$$+1 - 4 = ?$$

You would end up at –3 of course, so +1 – 4 = –3.

Now have a go at this one. If you were on floor +5 and went down 7 floors, where would you be then? How do we write that mathematically?

If you went down 7 floors, you would be at floor –2, so mathematically +5 – 7 = –2.

What about starting underground?

Suppose you were on the fourth floor underground, in other words –4, and went up 3 floors, where would you be then and how would this operation be written? Mathematically this is –4 + 3 = –1 so you end up on floor –1.

What about negatives minus negatives?

Let's say you were on the third floor below ground level and went down 5 floors. Where would you be then and how would this operation be written? Mathematically this would be –3 – 5 and this takes you to floor –8. So –3 – 5 –8.

Try some of these for yourself. Make sure you are clear about how to do this before you move on.

How to write directed numbers

In the earlier examples we have written 5 as +5. When we write numbers in mathematics, we either use positive or negative numbers. If we are using negative numbers, we must *always* write the number with a negative sign in front of it. So negative seven is always written as −7.

Positive numbers can be written as either a number with a positive sign in front or just as a number. So if a number, say five, is written as just 5 then it is automatically taken to mean +5. In other words if a number has no sign in front of it, it is *always* a positive number. Whenever you want to write a negative number, you must *always* write a negative sign in front of it.

So 5 and +5 are the same number. If you want to write negative five, you need to put a negative sign in front of it, so negative five is always written as −5.

Exercise 3.1
Calculate the value of each of these expressions.

1	$4 - 5 =$	**2**	$-3 - 5 =$	**3**	$9 - 17 =$
4	$-6 + 7 =$	**5**	$-15 + 17 =$	**6**	$12 - 17 =$
7	$5 - 12 =$	**8**	$22 - 9 =$	**9**	$-30 - 29 =$
10	$-7 - 9 =$				

Numbers and powers

Generally in mathematics we want to write things as simply as possible. Therefore there is a way of writing numbers that are multiplied by themselves.

Make sure you understand that any number on its own is to the power 1, so 7 is the same as 7^1. 9 is 9^1 and so on.

When a number is to the power 1, we do not need to write the 1 in. So any number written to the power 1 is just that number. So 144 is 144^1 and so on.

Suppose you want to write 3×3 – the shorthand way of writing this is 3^2. So 3^2 means 3×3 and clearly 3^2 must be 9 (and *not* 6 – it is 3×3 and not 2 lots of 3). 3^2 is said as 'three squared' or 'three to the power of two'.

The next one up in the sequence is 3^3 – we say this as 'three cubed' or 'three to the power three'. 3^3 is $3 \times 3 \times 3$. Now $3 \times 3 = 9$ and then 9×3 which is 27. So $3^3 = 27$.

For any power greater than 3, we say it is 'to the power of ...'. So, for example, 5^4 is said as 'five to the power of 4'. This worked out at $5 \times 5 \times 5 \times 5 = 625$. (Convince yourself of this).

Calculators are useful for working out expressions involving powers. On your calculator tap in '5'

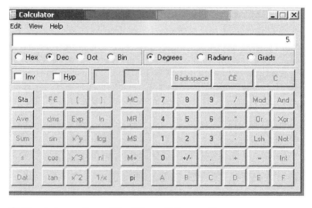

Screenshots courtesy of the Microsoft Corporation

Now you need to press either the x^y button or the y^x button. It depends on which type of calculator you have as to which button it will have.

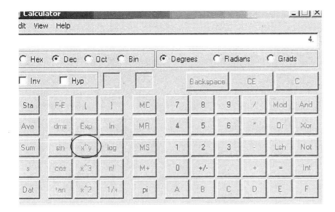

Screenshots courtesy of the Microsoft Corporation

Now press '4'. This tells the calculator that you want to work out 5^4. Mathematically this is called raising 5 to the power 4. Now press '=' and you will see the answer, 625.

Exercise 3.2
Write these numbers as powers and work them out.

1 $4 \times 4 =$ **2** $5 \times 5 \times 5 =$ **3** $4 \times 4 \times 4 =$

4 $9 \times 9 =$ **5** $7 \times 7 \times 7 =$ **6** $12 \times 12 =$

7 $3 \times 3 \times 3 \times 3 =$ **8** $13 \times 13 =$ **9** $14 \times 14 =$

10 $15 \times 15 =$

Now let's move into algebra

We have already discussed why algebra is important but it does need restating. The point of algebra is often lost on many people. The point is, that it is a tool that frees up our thinking. It is a way of writing rules that apply to all the occasions we are investigating. When we deal with numbers it only applies to that one particular case.

Say Mrs Jones has three bottles of milk every day. One way of working out the total cost is to write total cost 5 three times the cost of one bottle.

Immediately we are getting into algebra. This is a word equation – what if we were to do more 'shorthanding'.

Let's call the total cost T and the cost of one bottle c. Then we can rewrite the equation as

$T = 3c$.

Now we need to combine numbers and algebra. In algebra, we use the same rules that we use with numbers when working with powers.

Rule 1: Multiplying in algebra

When multiplying, you *add* the powers. So, for example,

$x \times x = x^2$.

This is because x on its own is x^1, so $x^1 \times x^1$ gives us x^{1+1} which is x^2.

Any variable (a variable is shown by a letter, like x or y) that does not have a power showing is automatically to the power 1. So y is y^1, m^1 is m and so on.

What about powers greater than 1?	The same rule applies – let's say we have to work out $m \times m^2$. As before, we add the powers so the answer is $m^{(1+2)}$ which is m^3.

Exercise 3.3

Work out the answers to these expressions – give your answers in the form x^y.

1	$w \times w^2$	2	$m^3 \times m^4$	3	$j^6 \times j^7$
4	$a^2 \times a^5$	5	$g^9 \times g^2$	6	$r \times r$
7	$e \times e^4$	8	$d \times d^5$	9	$s^5 \times s^6$
10	$y^3 \times y$				

Rule 2: Dividing in algebra

When you are dividing numbers involving powers, you *subtract* the powers. So, for example,

$$t^6 \div t^3 = t^{(6-3)} = t^3.$$

Remember, whatever the nature of the problem, when you are dividing the variables you subtract the powers.

Health warning 1	When we say add or subtract powers, we mean only if the variables are the same. So, for example, $b^3 \div b^2$ or $a^3 \times a^2$ are OK because we are dealing with just the b or just the a variable.
	If you had $b^3 \div a$ then there are two different variables and you cannot subtract the powers.
Health warning 2	Sometimes, you will see a division written like a fraction. So, for example, you might have $\dfrac{K^8}{K^3}$.
	This too is a division so you need to subtract the powers. So here, the answer is K^5.

Exercise 3.4

Express each of these in the form x^y.

1	$p^9 \div p^3$	**2**	$j^5 \div j^2$	**3**	$r^7 \div r^4$
4	$w^3 \div w^2$	**5**	$q^8 \div q^2$	**6**	$a^8 \div a^5$
7	$m^{12} \div m^6$	**8**	$h^{25} \div h^{24}$	**9**	$y^{60} \div y^{58}$
10	$n^2 \div n^{-4}$				

What about the power zero?

One way of thinking about this is to look at this pattern.

$$2^5 = 32$$

$$2^4 = 16$$

$$2^3 = 8$$

$$2^2 = 4$$

$$2^1 = 1$$

Any number to
the power zero
is one

Look at the pattern. As you go down the powers, the value halves each time. In other words 2^4 is half of 2^5. In the same way, 2^3 is half of 2^4 And so on down the line. So this means that 2^0 must be half of 2^1 so that means it must be 1.

So $10^0 = 1$ for example. Try it on your calculator – press '10' and then press your power key. You should find the answer is 1. The same is just as true in algebra. Say you had to work out $n^3 \div n^3$. The answer would be n^0 which we have just seen is 1. This makes sense if you think about it. What we are working out here is how many times n^3 divides into itself – clearly, the answer must be once.

Mathematics is a bit like a Windows operating system on a computer – whenever you learn to do something one way, there is usually an alternative way to do it. We could look at this calculation as $\dfrac{n^3}{n^3}$.

It is still a division and the powers are still subtracted, so the answer is still 1.

Tutorial

Progress questions

Set A

1 $4 - 6 =$ **2** $-3 - 7 =$ **3** $11 - 17 =$

4 $-6 + 1 =$ **5** $-15 + 13 =$ **6** $4 \times 4 =$

7 $5 \times 5 \times 5 =$ **8** $4 \times 4 \times 4 =$ **9** $9 \times 9 =$

10 $7 \times 7 \times 7 \times 7 =$

Set B

1 $w \times w^3 =$ **2** $m^3 \times m^5 =$ **3** $j^6 \times j^9 =$

4 $a^3 \times a^7 =$ **5** $g^9 \times g^3 =$ **6** $x^9 \times x^{-3} =$

7 $b^{-4} \times b^7 =$ **8** $c^{-1} \times c^3 =$ **9** $y^{-4} \times y^{-3} =$

10 $a^{-1} \times a^{-1}$

Set C

1 $p^9 \div p^2 =$ **2** $j^5 \div j^3 =$ **3** $r^7 \div r^3 =$

4 $w^3 \div w =$ **5** $q^8 \div q^3 =$ **6** $k^2 \div k^{-4} =$

7 $m^{-3} \div m^{-4} =$ **8** $b^{-6} \div b^7 =$ **9** $n \div n^{-4} =$

10 $a^{-3} \div a^7 =$

Discussion points

Describe how you feel about this chapter in your journal. *Do not* discuss this with another person yet. Make sure you describe your own feelings adequately and make them clear and unambiguous. At this stage do not be afraid of expressing concerns about your understanding – it is quite normal to feel unsure. Certainty comes from knowledge and success.

Practical assignment

Write out a worksheet of questions in the style of the questions in this chapter and provide the answers to your questions.

4 Patterns and Rules

One-minute overview

Patterns and rules are important in mathematics. It means that if we can see patterns then we can make predictions of what will happen. This is the real power of mathematics and why it is so very important.

Part of your mathematical education is to learn how to investigate. This chapter includes some simple investigations for you to learn the *method* of investigating. In fact they are very straightforward and you will probably be surprised at how easy they are to work out – but please remember it is the *method* that is important.

In this chapter you will learn to:
- make a statement of intent, to say what you are going to do;
- develop investigations to build up patterns in tables.

Statement of intent

You always start an investigation with a statement of intent. This is a statement that says what the investigation is about and how you intend to carry it out. In other words you would say,

> 'This investigation is about … In it I intend to investigate what happens when I do …'

For example, if you were given a scenario involving matchstick triangles:

Step 1: Make a statement of intent

This investigation is called Matchstick Triangles. I am going to investigate what happens when the sequence is increased, by counting the matches and the triangles.

Step 2: Collect some data

Now you would start looking at different lengths of sequences and you will have realised that you are looking at the number of triangles and the number of matches. Always make a table of results, in this case comparing the numbers of matches and triangles

Step 3: Work out the pattern

From the table work out what patterns you can see. You should to try to find an equation that links the number of matches and the number of triangles – in other words a piece of algebra that forms the general case. Think about it.

Triangles	1	2	3	4	5
Matches	3	5	7	9	11

(this row always goes up by two)

The fact that the number of matches always goes up by two means that this is a linear relationship (in other words, no powers greater than 1).

So now you have a hint – multiply the number of triangles (T) by 2 and what do you have to do then to get the number of matches (M)?

Brainwaves should be buzzing now

$$T \times 2 \ldots? = M$$

You've probably worked out that the relationship is

(the number of triangles $\times$ 2) + 1 = the number of matches.

In algebra this is written as

$$2T + 1 = M.$$

Don't forget, for each investigation you do make a statement of intent, draw a number of versions of the arrangement, make a table of results, state any patterns that you notice, and finally find the rule.

Investigation 1: Matchstick squares

Can you find a rule that links the number of squares with the number of matches?

Investigation 2: Houses

Can you find an algebraic link between the number of matches and the number of houses?

Investigation 3: Fishponds

Make the link between the number of fish and the number of slabs around the pond.

     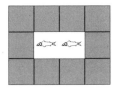

A one-fish pond   **A two-fish pond**

Investigation 4: Ells

In these L-shapes, compare the number (1, 2, 3) of the shape with the number of squares used. Remember – statement of intent, try out at least six, build a table and look for the rule.

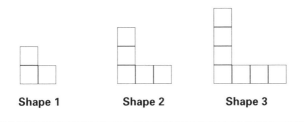

| Shape 1 | Shape 2 | Shape 3 |

By now you should be feeling a lot more comfortable with the idea of making generalisations in the form of simple equations. It is an important skill in mathematics.

What about non-linear relationships?

All the connections we have met at so far have been simple relationships called *linear relationships*. Linear relationships are algebraic expressions that when graphed form a straight line.

Now look at these results from a start–end game.

Start	1	2	3	4	5	6
End	1	4	9	16	25	36

Have you spotted the connection here? Look back at Chapter 2 if you are not sure – we have discussed these numbers before.

Now look at the first differences in the end number row – here they are again.

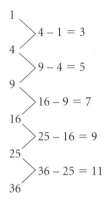

$$4 - 1 = 3$$
$$9 - 4 = 5$$
$$16 - 9 = 7$$
$$25 - 16 = 9$$
$$36 - 25 = 11$$

So here the first differences are all different – they are 3, 5, 7, 9 and 11. But clearly there is a pattern here. We can easily predict that the next first difference in this sequence will be 13, and if you add 13 to 36 you get 49 as the end number, and obviously 7 as the start number. So we must be on to something here – *but* what do we multiply the start number by to get the end number?

Before we can answer this question, we need to do a little more digging. Let's look at the first differences again. They are 3, 5, 7, 9, 11, 13 ... Let's see if it helps if we find the second differences.

$$5 - 3 = 2$$
$$7 - 5 = 2$$
$$9 - 7 = 2$$
$$11 - 9 = 2$$
$$13 - 11 = 2$$

This tells us something – in fact it tells us that the start number is multiplied by itself to make the end number. What is the name of the operation where we multiply a number by itself? It is called squaring the number – so in this sequence we square the start number

start number × start number = ?

This is unwieldy so let's use some algebra – letting s represent the start number

$s \times s = ?$

But this is also not the best final form. The best way of writing 's squared' is

$s^2 = ?$

OK. So now let's look at the numbers we used in this start–end game.

$1^2 = 1 \times 1 = \mathbf{1}$
$2^2 = 2 \times 2 = \mathbf{4}$
$3^2 = 3 \times 3 = \mathbf{9}$
$4^2 = 4 \times 4 = \mathbf{16}$

...

The numbers in bold type are the end numbers (e) in the original sequence. So the relationship, or rule, is $s^2 = e$

Don't be too surprised if this is not too clear at the moment – you may need to go through it a couple of times. To help make this idea of non-linear relationships clearer let's look at another investigation.

The patterns below are made up of matchsticks. Again we can make a table of values and look at the differences. As always, the first step is to try some out and then move on to collect data and finally look for a relationship.

Pattern 1   **Pattern 2**   **Pattern 3**

Look at how these patterns are made up. In the first square we have 4 matches making a 1×1 square. In the second square we have 12 matchsticks making a 2×2 square. In the third square we have 24 matchsticks, giving us a 3×3 square.

The next stage here is to collect some data.

Pattern number (n)	Number of matchsticks (m)	First differences
1	4	
		8
2	12	
		12
3	24	
		16
4	40	
		20
5	60	
		24
6	84	

When we look at the differences we spot an immediate problem – they are not all the same. This means that there is not a linear relationship. (Remember, for a linear relationship all the first differences must be the same.)

In cases like this it is important to look at the second differences.

1st differences	8	12	16	20	24
2nd differences	4	4	4	4	

Here the second differences are all the same and they are a multiple of 2. This is an important clue for this investigation – it means the relationship must be quadratic (one in which the highest power is 2). To find the rule, let's look at this table. The first row shows that there are 4 matchsticks in pattern 1. If the pattern number (n) is squared we get 1. If we then double this number we get 2.

n	m	n^2	$2n^2$
1	4	1	2
2	12	4	8
3	24	9	18
4	40	16	32
5	60	25	50

Look at the column headed $2n^2$. Can you see that we have to add a multiple of 2 to the numbers in this column to get the number of matchsticks (m)?

The number in the $2n^2$ column in the first row is important. Notice that we have to add a multiple of 2 to the numbers in this column, to get the number of matchsticks. In the first row, the number in the $2n^2$ column is 2. If we add 2×1 to this we get 4, which is the number of matchsticks in the m column.

In the second row, the number in the $2n^2$ column is 8. Add 2 $\times$ 2 and you get 12, which is the number of matchsticks. And so it goes on.

This means that the rule connecting the number of matchsticks and the diagram number must be

$m = 2n^2 + 2n$

where m is the number of matchsticks and n is the pattern number. In pattern 3 for example,

$$m = (2 \times 3^2) + (2 \times 3)$$
$$= 18 + 6$$
$$= 24.$$

Work through some of the other rows to convince yourself. Then try convincing another person.

What about all of those *x*'s and *y*'s?

Algebra seems full of *x*'s and *y*'s where we have used mainly *s* and *e* or *m* and *n* for our equations so far. In fact $s^2 = e$ and $x^2 = y$ are equivalent equations. They describe the same operation, so instead of using *s* and *e* we could easily use *x* and *y*.

Here is another straightforward start–end table.

Start	1	2	3	4	5
End	1	8	27	64	125

Working out the first differences it is immediately obvious that they are different.

$$8-1 = 7, \quad 27-8 = 19, \quad 64-27 = 37, \quad 125-64 = 61.$$

Now let's look at the second differences.

$$19-7 = 12, \quad 37-19 = 18, \quad 61-37 = 24.$$

Again these are all different. Let's work out the third differences.

$$18-12 = 6, \quad 24-8 = 6.$$

They are all 6.

So this cannot be a linear (power 1) relationship or a quadratic (squared) relationship. In fact it must be more than that. So let's try a cubic relationship. We discussed cubic in Chapter 2 so if you are not sure have a quick look back now. Here's a cubic relationship.

$$1^3 = 1 \times 1 \times 1 = \mathbf{1}$$
$$2^3 = 2 \times 2 \times 2 = \mathbf{8}$$
$$3^3 = 3 \times 3 \times 3 = \mathbf{27}$$

So clearly the relationship in the start–end game we are investigating here is cubic and, in fact, it is the series of cube numbers. Writing this algebraically this gives us the relationship

$$s^3 = e$$

Note that this could be written as $x^3 = y$

Investigation 5: Frogs

The big frogs have to get to where the small frogs are, and the small frogs to where the big frogs are – but there are some rules to be obeyed.

● Only one frog can move at a time.

● A frog can hop onto the stone between the frogs.

● A frog can hop over another frog into an empty space.

The problem to solve is, with three frogs on each side, what is the minimum number of moves needed to get all the big frogs to where the small frogs are, and all the small frogs to where the big frogs are?

What about 4 frogs on each side? 5 frogs? 6 frogs? 10 frogs? Clearly it would be useful to have a relationship between the number of frogs and the number of moves.

Can you find an algebraic relationship (rule) that connects the number of frogs on each side with the number of moves? You could start with small numbers and then successively add one frog to each side.

You could extend this investigation by changing the rules. What if there are different numbers of frogs on each side? What about a different number of stones between the big frogs and the small frogs?

Tutorial

Answer the following questions in your journal.

1 What is a linear relationship ?

2 What is a quadratic relationship?

3 What is a cubic relationship?

4 Explain how the method of first differences works.

5 Explain how we can spot a quadratic relationship using the method of second differences.

Discussion points

In your journal write down these steps in completing an investigation and add an example investigation of your own.

1 Make a statement of intent.

2 Collect data and build up a table of results.

3 Use the method of differences to establish a relationship between the variables.

Practical assignment

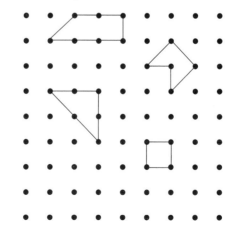

Investigate the relationship (rule) in the following situation.

1 Make some dotty shapes with no dots inside – like the ones in the diagram.

2 Find the area of each shape and the number of dots on its perimeter.

3 Make a table of results with area in one column and the number of dots in the other.

4 Label each column with a letter – either *x* or *y*.

5 Formulate an equation that describes the relationship.

6 Generalise – find a rule that connects the number of dots on the perimeter and the area.

7 Now do the same for shapes with one dot inside and two dots and so on.

How to Solve Linear Equations

Equations are statements written in the language of algebra. They are algebraic expressions and contain the '=' symbol just once, meaning the two sides must be equal. A useful skill is to have is to be able to rearrange equations to calculate the value of a variable. *Variable* is a term used for a quantity that can vary – in algebra variables are represented by letters. Think of the different equations you have ever met and you will have often used letters like x and y, but the actual values they represent will have been different in different circumstances – in other words the values will have varied, that is why we call them variables.

In this chapter, you will learn:

■ how to solve an equation with an unknown on one side;

■ how to solve an equation with an unknown on both sides;

■ how to solve an equation with an unknown on both sides and a negative coefficient;

■ how to solve equations with brackets;

■ how to solve equations with fractions.

What is an equation?

An equation is an algebraic expression which contains the $=$ symbol just once, meaning that the two sides must be equal. So $x + 4 = 10$ is an equation – it reads as 'an unknown number + 4 gives the answer 10'. Clearly that number must be 6.

The important thing is to learn the *method* for solving

equations, because this will form the foundation for tackling harder equations.

Note that it is standard practice when writing a set of equations on successive lines to ensure that the equal signs line up underneath each other.

How to solve an equation with an unknown on one side

We will call this a *type one* equation. Let's look at the example we just used. We know that the answer is 6, but how do we get there?

$$x + 4 = 10$$

We have already agreed that this means 'a number + 4 = 10'. If we take 4 away from the left-hand side it will leave us with just the number x. But to keep the equation in balance, we need to take 4 from the right-hand side as well. So the next line is

$$x + 4 - 4 = 10 - 4$$

On the left-hand side, $4 - 4 = 0$, so that must mean we are only left with the x. So the next line is

$$x = 6$$

and this is the final answer.

It is always a good idea to do a check at the end. If we put the 6 back into the original equation we get $6 + 4 = 10$ and we know we have solved the equation correctly.

Review	Look at what we have done. The left-hand side had a +4 so we subtracted 4 from the left-hand side and therefore had to subtract 4 from the right-hand side. We 'undid' the equation by subtracting 4 from both sides. Manipulating an equation like this leaves the unknown on its own on one side of the equation. In algebra this is known as *isolating the variable*.

Try this one.

$$y + 7 = 21$$

Since we have a +7 on the left, we need to undo the left-hand side by taking 7 away. This will leave us with the y. But we must also take 7 away from the right-hand side.

$$y + 7 - 7 = 21 - 7$$
$$y = 14$$

Check: substitute the final answer into the original equation. Do this by taking out the y, putting in the 14 and then making the judgement as to whether it makes sense or not. Substituting gives $14 + 7 = 21$, so we know that $y = 14$ must be correct.

Exercise 5.1
Work out the value of the variable in each of these expressions.

1 $z + 5 = 10$	**2** $y + 8 = 19$	**3** $v + 8 = 15$
4 $m + 4 = 7$	**5** $f + 8 = 12$	**6** $d + 15 = 35$
7 $a + 4 = 16$	**8** $r + 23 = 51$	**9** $a + 20 = 119$
10 $p + 9 = 90$		

What about equations with subtractions in them?

In the examples above, we undid an equation by subtracting from both sides. This was because the equations were all of the form

an unknown + a number = another number.

Example 1
Let's look at the equation

$$x - 7 = 15.$$

Here the form is different – it is

an unknown – a number = another number.

To undo this type of equation you need to add instead of subtract. So, for example, look at the equation

$x - 7 = 15.$

Now add 7 to both sides,

$x - 7 + 7 = 15 + 7.$

Since $-7 + 7 = 0$, the equation now becomes

$x = 22.$

Check: Putting 22 in to the original equation, we get $22 - 7 = 15$, just what we wanted. So $x = 22$ must be the correct answer.

Example 2

$y - 9 = 27.$

Undo the equation by adding 9 to both sides

$$y - 9 + 9 = 27 + 9$$
$$y = 36.$$

Check: $36 - 9 = 27$. So we know that $y = 36$ is correct.

Example 3

This one has a slight twist.

$14 - k = 20.$

This can often cause panic because of the way the equation is presented. However, with a bit of clear thinking this does not have to be a problem. As before, we first 'tidy up' the numbers. To do this we subtract 14 from both sides.

$$14 - k - 14 = 20 - 14$$
$$-k = 6.$$

Multiplying throughout an equation by –1

Think about equations like

$-y = 5$

We don't want –y, we want y. To do this the technique used is to multiply throughout by –1.

$-y \times -1 = y$ and $5 \times -1 = -5$

So after multiplying by –1, the equation becomes

$y = -5$

This is a useful technique for changing equations from a negative form to a positive form.

Returning to the problem – we multiply throughout by –1 to get

$k = -6$.

Check: putting this into the original equation gives $14 - (-6) = 14 + 6 = 20$ so we know we are correct.

Exercise 5.2

Work out the value of the variable in each of these expressions.

1 $x - 7 = 30$	**2** $v - 8 = 19$	**3** $c - 6 = 9$
4 $m - 30 = 17$	**5** $k - 40 = 15$	**6** $a - 8 = 12$
7 $l - 9 = 45$	**8** $d - 60 = 50$	**9** $q - 90 = 100$
10 $n - 25 = 250$	**11** $12 - k = 10$	**12** $14 - f = 20$
13 $10 - 10k = 100$	**14** $17h - 6 = 28$	**15** $6 - 12f = 18$

What about equations with multiplications in them?

Multiplication in algebra is indicated by putting two terms side by side. So $3x$ means $3 \times x$. At this stage it doesn't matter what x is, we are simply trying to work out a method for undoing the multiplication. Remember when we did earlier *type one* equations, we undid addition by subtracting. This works because, for example, $3 - 3 = 0$.

So can we make it work with multiplication? Pick any number and multiply it by 4. Now divide your answer by 4 – what happens? Does this always happen? Make sure that you convince yourself, before you go any further.

How does this work in an equation?

Look at $3x = 12$. Again we have picked a simple equation because we want you to be clear on the *method* we are going to use. Clearly this equation is saying

'3 multiplied by an unknown number $= 12$'

So obviously the unknown number must be 4 – but we need to understand how to do this algebraically.

We have already said that $\div$ and $\times$ are opposites. Let's look at this in action.

$$12 \times 4 = 48$$
$$\frac{48}{4} = 12$$

So, dividing by the same thing that we multiplied by allows us to undo a multiplication. Here we multiplied 12 by 4 and then divided the result by 4 – leaving the 12 unchanged. Try some more of these out for yourself – convince yourself first and then convince another person.

How does this work in algebra?

It is just the same principle. Look at this term, $\dfrac{3x}{3}$.

$3x$ is being divided by 3 and clearly this does not change the value of x, so we can literally cross the 3s out.

$$\frac{\cancel{3}x}{\cancel{3}}$$

This leaves us with x. This is the called the method of *cancelling* – it *only* works when you are *multiplying* (or dividing).

Example 1

So let's go back to our starting example, $3x = 12$. The technique is to divide both sides by whatever is in front of the unknown (variable) – this is called the coefficient of x. So here we divide both sides by 3 and the equation becomes

$$\frac{\cancel{3}x}{\cancel{3}} = \frac{12}{3}.$$

The 3s on the left-hand side cancel and so $x = 4$.

Notice how we divided both sides of the equation by the same thing, using the golden rule that you never operate on one side of the equation without doing exactly the same thing on the other side.

Don't forget the check: putting $x = 4$ into $3x$ we get the answer 12 – just as it should be if we have done things correctly,

Example 2

The equation is $5y = 100$ so we divide both sides by the number in front of the unknown, in this case 5

$$\frac{\cancel{5}y}{\cancel{5}} = \frac{100}{5}.$$

The 5s on the left-hand side cancel and since $100 \div 5 = 20$, then $y = 20$.

Check: Putting $y = 20$ into $5y$ gives 100.

Exercise 5.3

Work out the value of the variable in each of these expressions.

1 $6y = 36$	**2** $7m = 42$	**3** $18n = 36$
4 $9y = 27$	**5** $14y = 28$	**6** $12t = 144$

7 $10u = 55$ **8** $100r = 100$ **9** $25f = 50$

10 $4d = 16$

What about equations with divisions in them?

Just as with multiplication, we have to do the opposite. Here we have to multiply to undo the equation. For example, with

$\dfrac{x}{4} = 7$ we multiply both sides by 4

$\dfrac{x \times 4}{4} = 7 \times 4.$

Now, the 4s on the left-hand side cancel,

$\dfrac{x \times \cancel{4}}{\cancel{4}} = 7 \times 4,$ and we are left with $x = 28.$

Check: putting $x = 28$ into $\frac{x}{4}$ gives 7 – just as it should do.

Once again, convince yourself about this – make sure you understand it. Try talking it through with another person – it really does help you to understand the mathematics.

Exercise 5.4

Work out the value of the variable in each of these expressions.

1 $\dfrac{x}{3} = 9$ **2** $\dfrac{t}{7} = 3$ **3** $\dfrac{m}{5} = 8$

4 $\dfrac{y}{6} = 8$ **5** $\dfrac{t}{12} = 5$ **6** $\dfrac{a}{2} = 2$

7 $\dfrac{y}{2} = 3$ **8** $\dfrac{p}{3} = 11$ **9** $\dfrac{y}{6} = 15$

10 $\dfrac{k}{2} = 5$

You now have all the skills needed to solve simple equations with one unknown. What you may not have realised yet is that they occur in all sorts of combinations. For example,

$2x + 4 = 7.$

Here you have to undo the addition and then undo the multiplication between the 2 and the *x*. So, in stages, taking 4 from both sides

$$2x + 4 - 4 = 7 - 4$$

The bolded part shows the original equation – all we have done is take 4 from both sides. This gives

$$2x = 3$$

Now undo the 2*x* by dividing both sides by 2

$$\frac{\cancel{2}x}{\cancel{2}} = \frac{3}{2} \text{ and so } x = 1.5.$$

Check: putting *x* = 1.5 in 2*x* + 4 produces 7 – just as it should do.

Exercise 5.5

Work out the value of the variable in each of these expressions.

1	2*x* + 5 = 9	**2**	4*x* + 6 = 14	**3**	5*f* + 9 = 54
4	5*x* + 7 = 37	**5**	6*r* + 8 = 50	**6**	8*t* + 9 = 17
7	9*p* + 1 = 82	**8**	7*r* + 1 = 15	**9**	8*y* + 6 = 70
10	6*r* + 4 = 40				

How to solve equations containing negative numbers

For example 4*x* – 13 = –1, but don't worry – you have already seen these before. Remember, undo the equation by doing the opposite and always do exactly the same thing to both sides of the equation.

So for 4*x* – 13 = –1, add 13 to both sides, to undo the –13 and we get

$$4x - 13 + 13 = -1 + 13$$
$$4x = 12.$$

Look at what has happened, we have changed an equation from a type we didn't know about, to one we do know about. We have seen this type before. So now you just need to solve this in the same way as you did earlier. Have a go at it first and then check your answer with the one below.

You should have found that $x = 3$.

Check: putting $x = 3$ into $4x - 13$ gives -1, just as it should do.

Exercise 5.6

Work out the value of the variable in each of these expressions.

1	$2x - 3 = 1$	**2**	$4x - 8 = 28$	**3**	$5f - 5 = 30$
4	$5x - 10 = 25$	**5**	$6r - 6 = 30$	**6**	$8t - 7 = 1$
7	$9p - 1 = 17$	**8**	$7r - 1 = 20$	**9**	$8y - 2 = 78$
10	$6r - 4 = 50$				

How to solve equations with an unknown on both sides of the equation

Remember what we said in the last section, change the equation into a type you are already familiar with and know how to solve.

Look at this equation – it has an x on both sides

$$4x + 4 = x + 16.$$

Tackle it by undoing the x term with the lowest coefficient. Since x is smaller than $4x$, undo this one first. So it becomes

$$4x + 4 - x = x + 16 - x$$
$$3x + 4 = 16.$$

Now you have it in a form that you should recognise and know how to solve. So have a go and solve it now – then check with the answer below.

You should have found that $x = 4$.

Check: putting $x = 4$ into $4x + 4 = x + 16$ gives $20 = 20$, which is fine.

Remember, this is all to do with changing equations from a form that you don't know what to do with straightaway into a form that you are confident with and have the techniques to tackle.

Health wrning

Some students develop the habit of writing equations as they think. Remember, you only use one equals sign on each level of working. For example, presented with $x + 3 = 4$ they say take 3 away from both sides, so that $x + 3 - 3 = 4 - 3$.

So far everything is fine except this is when the brain goes into overdrive. They recognise that $4 - 3 = 1$, and so that $x = 1$. But the way they write it down is wrong. They stick another $=$ sign on the end and get $x + 3 - 3 = 4 - 3 = 1$.

The correct way to write this calculation out is

$$x + 3 = 4$$
$$x + 3 - 3 = 4 - 3$$
$$x = 1.$$

Exercise 5.7
Work out the value of the variable in each of these expressions.

1   $5x - 4 = 4x + 1$ 2 $9y + 17 = 14y + 7$

3   $4t + 5 = 6t - 3$ 4 $8a + 5 = 3a + 50$

5   $6y + 7 = 7y$

What about brackets?

Brackets are commonly used in mathematics. Usually brackets tell you to deal with the numbers inside the brackets first. So, say you had $3 \times (4 + 5)$. This means do the $4 + 5$ sum first, and then multiply the answer by 3. So the answer you should get is 27.

But in algebra things are done slightly differently! In algebra brackets mean that you have to multiply. So $3(x+4)$ means do $3 \times x$ first and then do $+3 \times 4$ giving $3x + 12$. In other words,

$3(x +4) = 3x + 12.$

This is called *expanding brackets*.

Exercise 5.7
Expand these brackets.

1	$8(c + 6)$	2	$2(a + 3)$	3	$6(t + 5)$
4	$5(u - 8)$	5	$3(r - 9)$	6	$6(y - 7)$
7	$4(y - 5)$	8	$3(2t - 6)$	9	$5(7y - 6)$
10	$7(7t + 7)$				

How to solve equations with fractions

This topic was looked at this earlier in this chapter, but we will revise what we have done in order to make sure you are comfortable with the *method*.

The denominator is the lower part of the fraction. You need to think of denominators as dividers.

So to undo the division when the unknown is in the denominator you need to multiply. Look at this example.

$$\frac{4}{x} = 5$$

This reads as '4 divided by an unknown equals 5'. The rule is to multiply both sides of the equation by what is in the denominator. So here

$$\frac{4}{x} \times x = 5 \times x$$

Look at what happens to the left-hand side

$$\frac{4}{\cancel{x}} \times \cancel{x} = 5 \times x$$

The x's cancel and notice what this does– it changes the equation to a form we have already worked on. Now the equation reads

$$4 = 5x$$

and all we have to do solve it use the rules we met earlier. Divide both sides by 5 and do the cancelling

$$\frac{4}{5} = \frac{\cancel{5}x}{\cancel{5}}$$

So that gives us $\dfrac{4}{5} = x$ or $x = \dfrac{4}{5}$.

Unsure about cancelling?	Look at this, $3x = 7$. This reads '3 times an unknown number equals 7'. We don't want 3 times the unknown, we want the unknown on its own. So we divide both sides by 3 $\quad \dfrac{3x}{3} = \dfrac{7}{3}$

We are now multiplying and dividing the x by the same number. What happens when you multiply and divide a number by the same number? You are left with the original number. That's why we can cancel the threes on the left-hand side leaving x on its own.

So $x = \dfrac{7}{3}$

Tutorial

1 $k + 7 = 10$ **2** $y + 9 = 19$ **3** $v + 2 = 15$

4 $m + 3 = 7$ **5** $f + 7 = 12$ **6** $x - 10 = 30$

7 $v - 7 = 19$ **8** $c - 8 = 9$ **9** $m - 31 = 17$

10 $k - 41 = 15$ **11** $7y = 49$ **12** $7m = 35$

13 $6n = 36$ **14** $9y = 27$ **15** $14y = 28$

16 $\dfrac{x}{3} = 9$ **17** $\dfrac{m}{5} = 8$ **18** $\dfrac{t}{7} = 3$

19 $\dfrac{y}{6} = 8$ **20** $\dfrac{t}{12} = 5$ **21** $8(c + 6) = 22$

22 $2(a + 3) = 18$ **23** $6(t + 5) = 51$ **24** $5(u - 8) = 45$

25 $3(r - 9) = 27$

Discussion point

Explain the techniques you have met in this chapter to another person. Convince yourself first and then convince them.

Study tip

Use your journal to record an example of each of these techniques in action. Write out a model solution on the left-hand side of the page with a black pen, and then use a red pen to write instructions on the right-hand side. You could use this as material to help the explanation suggested above.

Brackets and Factors

One-minute overview

In this chapter we are going to look at how to use brackets and factors. The first part will deal with expanding brackets. Then we will look at factors.

In this chapter you will learn:
- about simple expansion of brackets and factorising;
- about the difference of two squares;
- how to factorise quadratic equations;
- how to complete the square as a mechanism for factorising;
- how change the subject of a formula;
- how to deal with algebraic fractions.

How to expand brackets

Brackets in algebra often cause confusion – but there is nothing to fear here. Let's look at a simple example. Suppose we want to expand $(x + 4)(x + 3)$. We can use the rectangle diagram to help.

Now look at the area of each of the rectangles. The top left rectangle is actually a square. We know this because both

sides have the same length (x). OK, so how do we calculate
the area of a square? We use the simple formula, area = l^2.
So the area of the top left square is x^2.

Now let's do the same with the top right rectangle – you
should find that the area is $4x$. The bottom left rectangle
comes out at $3x$ and the bottom right comes out at 12 (4×3).

x^2	$4x$
$3x$	12

We can now put these separate areas together as
$x^2 + 4x + 3x + 12$. Notice that the two middle terms are like
terms and so can be added together. So the final answer is
$x^2 + 7x + 12$.

This means that

$$(x + 4)(x + 3) = x^2 + 7x + 12$$

After some practice, you will find that you will be able to do
this expansion without the diagrams –but don't worry about
using them at this stage. If they help you to learn, that is all
that matters.

Pause	Use your journal to make a note of what we have just done. Draw the diagram and annotate it. Use colour on the diagram – this stimulates the brain.
	In your own words explain what we have done and how we used the diagram to get to the final answer.
	Remember, convince yourself, then convince someone else

A word on like and unlike terms

In trials for this book, we found that some people, mainly adults who have missed out on parts of their education, had difficulty with the idea of *like* and *unlike* terms. In algebra, like terms are terms that are the same and can be operated on. By 'operated' we mean you can add, subtract, multiply or divide. This is not as strange as it might first appear. In real life, you cannot add hens and elephants. If you have three hens and six elephants, you cannot combine them to get nine hen-elephants nor nine elephant-hens.

Like terms

In algebra we use the noun 'variable' to apply to values in equations – we show these variables as letters of the alphabet. So, in short, you can add or subtract, multiply or divide *letters* that are the same. If the letters are not the same you cannot operate on them. So in algebra

$$a + a = 2a$$
$$b + b + b = 3b.$$

Unlike terms

Notice that uppercase letters and lowercase letters *do not* represent the same variable – so B is not the same as b. Similarly x^2 is not the same as x (think about it, $x^2 = x \times x$).

When you multiply unlike variables, they are written side by side, so $x \times y$ is written as xy, and a divided by b is usually written as the fraction $\frac{a}{b}$.

Multiplying by 1

We do not write $1x$ or $1a$ or $1b$. If the variable is a letter on its own, then it is automatically taken as just one of them – so $1b$ should just be written as b, $1a$ should just be written as a and so on.

Make a journal entry on like and unlike terms. Be clear in your own mind what these mean and how to use this information in your own algebra.

Here is another example showing how to expand brackets using $(x+1)(x+3)$.

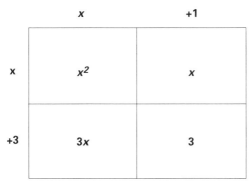

So $(x + 1)(x + 3) = x^2 + x + 3x + 3$, but remember we need to tidy up the middle two terms. So

$$(x +1)(x + 3) = x^2 + 4x + 3.$$

Exercise 6.1
Expand the brackets and simplify these expressions.

1 $(x + 2)(x + 3)$ 2 $(x + 1)(x + 5)$

3 $(y + 3)(y +4)$ 4 $(x - 2)(x + 5)$

5 $(x + 5)(x -3)$ 6 $(m + 7)(m - 3)$

7 $(v + 4)(v - 3)$ 8 $(z - 8)(z - 7)$

9 $(a - 7)(a - 5)$ 10 $(d + 6)(d + 7)$

Expanding brackets with coefficients greater than one

The coefficient is the number in front of the letter, so c on its own has a coefficient of 1, as indeed does x, y or any other variable on its own. In this section we will be dealing with expanding expressions such as $(4x + 5)(x -2)$.

You have a go at this and compare your answer with ours below.

OK. how well did you get on? The secret here is to expand the x's first and then do the numbers. First, multiply the $4x$ in the first bracket by everything in the *second* bracket. That gives two terms, $4x \times x$ and $4x \times -2$.

Then multiply the $+5$ in the first bracket by everything in the *second* bracket. That gives two more terms, $+5 \times x$ and $+5 \times -2$.

Adding these new terms together gives $4x^2 - 8x + 5x - 10$. As in the earlier examples we tidy up the middle two terms giving the final expansion

$$4x^2 - 3x - 10.$$

How did you get on? Do you agree with our solution?

Pause	Use your journal to make a note of what we have just done. Draw the diagram and annotate it. Use colour on the diagram as this stimulates the brain. In your own words explain what we have done and how we used the diagram to get to the final answer
	Remember, convince yourself, then convince someone else

Exercise 6.2

Expand the brackets and simplify these expressions.

1   $(2x + 1)(x - 4)$ 2 $(3x + 4)(x - 1)$

3   $(3d - 4)(4d - 3)$ 4 $(3f - 5)(4f + 6)$

5   $(7g - 5)(g - 6)$ 6 $(4 - x)(6 - x)$

7   $(6 - y)(7 - y)$ 8 $(9 + t)(t^2 + 4)$

9   $(14 - y)(12 + 2y)$ 10 $3(4y - 3)(5y + 4)$

Expanding squares

Here is another type of expression which includes brackets, $(x + 5)^2$. How is this type of expression expanded?

Squaring means multiplying something by itself. So $(x + 5)^2$ means $(x + 5)(x + 5)$ – so we work this out exactly in the same way that we worked out the earlier type of bracket expression. Therefore,

$$(x+5)^2 = (x+5)(x+5)$$
$$= x^2 + 5x + 5x + 25$$
$$= x^2 + 10x + 25.$$

Exercise 6.3

Expand the brackets and simplify these expressions.

1   $(x + 4)^2$ 2 $(f + 5)^2$

3   $(x - 3)^2$ 4 $(d + 7)^2$

5   $(m + 2)^2$ 6 $(g - 3)^2$

7   $(x + 1)^2 + (x - 2)^2$ 8 $(k + 6)^2 + (k + 8)^2$

9   $(y - 4)^2 + (y + 6)^2$ 10 $(x + 2)^2 + (3x - 4)^2$

Exercise 6.4

Expand the brackets and simplify these expressions.

1   $(x + 3)^2$ 2 $(x + 1)^2$

3   $(x - 5)^2$ 4 $(3x + 2)^2$

5   $(4y + 1)^2$ 6 $4(x + 6)^2$

7   $2(x + 1)^2$ 8 $6(x + 3)^2$

9   $5(x + 2)^2$ 10 $5(y + 7)^2$

Solving equations by expanding brackets

Using the ideas about how to expand brackets that we have discussed in this chapter, we can solve certain types of equations. Look at this example

$$x^2 + 4 = (x + 1)(x + 3)$$

Here we need to expand the right-hand side of the equation, then we need to tidy up the equation by collecting like terms. Then we need to change the equation into a form that we have already worked with.

Step 1: Expand the brackets

$$x^2 + 4 = (x+1)(x+3)$$
$$= x^2 + 3x + x + 3$$
$$= x^2 + 4x + 3$$

Step 2: Get a different form we can work with

Subtract x^2 from both sides,

$$x^2 + 4 - x^2 = x^2 + 4x + 3 - x^2$$
$$4 = 4x + 3$$

Step 3: Work out the value of the unknown

Subtract 3 from both sides

$$4 - 3 = 4x + 3 - 3$$
$$1 = 4x$$

Divide both sides by 4

$$\frac{1}{4} = \frac{\cancel{4}x}{\cancel{4}}$$
$$\frac{1}{4} = x$$

Check: putting $x = \frac{1}{4}$ into the original equation,

$$x^2 + 4 = (x+1)(x+3)$$

$$\left(\frac{1}{4}\right)^2 + 4 = \left(\frac{1}{4}+1\right)\left(\frac{1}{4}+3\right)$$

$$\frac{1}{16} + 4 = \frac{5}{4} \times \frac{13}{4}$$

$$4\frac{1}{16} = \frac{65}{16} = 4\frac{1}{16}.$$

The fact that the two sides are equal means that our solution to the equation must be correct.

Solving equations with brackets

Now that you know how to expand brackets you can solve some simple equations.

Example 1
Solve $x^2 + 29 = (x + 1)(x + 4)$

The first step is to expand the right-hand side

$$x^2 + 29 = x^2 + 4x + x + 4$$
$$= x^2 + 5x + 4$$

Now let's solve the equation. To start with we will take x^2 from both sides.

$$x^2 + 29 - x^2 = x^2 + 5x + 4 - x^2$$
$$29 = 5x + 4$$

Now take 4 from both sides

$$29 - 4 = 5x + 4 - 4$$
$$25 = 5x$$

Now divide both sides by 5

$$\frac{25}{5} = \frac{\cancel{5}x}{\cancel{5}}$$
$$5 = x$$

Just for the sake of convention we need to reverse this. In other words, it is usual to see the unknown on the left-hand side of the equation. So the solution is

$x = 5$.

Check: putting $x = 5$ in the original equation gives

$$5^2 + 29 = (5+1)(5+4)$$
$$25 + 29 = (6) \times (9)$$
$$54 = 54$$

Since both sides of the equation give 54 then we must have the correct solution to the equation.

Example 2

Solve $3x^2 + 21 = (x + 7)(3x + 5)$.

As before we expand the right-hand side and tidy up by collecting like terms.

$$3x^2 + 21 = 3x^2 + 5x + 21x + 35$$
$$= 3x^2 + 26x + 35$$

Here we need to remember that x^2 terms and x terms are *not* like terms so they cannot be added to or subtracted from each other.

The next step is to undo the smallest number – this is +21, so we subtract 21 from both sides of the equation.

$$3x^2 + 21 - 21 = 3x^2 + 26x + 35 - 21$$
$$3x^2 = 3x^2 + 26x + 14$$

Now subtract $3x^2$ from both sides

$$3x^2 - 3x^2 = 3x^2 + 26x + 14 - 3x^2$$
$$0 = 26x + 14$$

Remember the technique we are using in these examples – we have changed the equation from a form that we did not know how to work on to a form we feel more comfortable with.

Now take 14 from both sides

$$26x + 14 - 14 = 0 - 14$$
$$26x = -14$$

Notice we have written the equation in the more conventional way. Now divide both sides by 26

$$\frac{26x}{26} = \frac{-14}{26}$$
$$x = -\frac{7}{13}.$$

We'll leave you to do the checking!

Exercise 6.5

Expand the brackets, simplify and solve these equations.

1 $x^2 + 1 = (x + 1)(x + 5)$

2 $x^2 + 9 = (x + 3)(x - 1)$

3 $x^2 - 7 = (x - 7)(x + 3)$

4 $(y - 2)(y + 3) = (y - 7)(y + 7)$

5 $(y - 4)(y + 3) = y^2 + 2y - 14$

6 $x(2x + 7) = 2x^2 - 8$

7 $x^2 - (x + 1)^2 = 9x - 2$

8 $(2x - 1)(x + 3) = (2x - 3)(x - 1)$

9 $x^2 - 4 = 0$

10 $x^2 - 9 = 0$

The last two questions in this exercise may prove a little challenging. If this is so, you need to look at the *difference of two squares*, which is covered later in this chapter.

Factors and factorising

Factorising is the opposite of expanding brackets. It is the process of identifying the factors that make up a term – we are 'putting brackets in'.

Example 1

How do we factorise $6y + 4$?

First we need to look for the terms that multiply together to make $6y$ and then 4. Looking for the largest number that goes into both 6 and 4, it turns out to be 2. So we now have

$$6y + 4 = 2(? + ?)$$

Now, what do we need to multiply 2 by, to make $6y$? That must be $3y$ so we have the first term inside the bracket

$$6y + 4 = 2(3y + ?)$$

Now we need to work out the last term in the bracket. Ask yourself 'what do I need to multiply the 2 outside the bracket with to generate the $+4$?' Obviously it must be $+2$, so that gives us the final term and the answer.

$$6y + 4 = 2(3y + 2).$$

Notice that we have reversed the expansion technique that we looked at earlier in this chapter.

Example 2

How do we factorise $3xy + 6y^2$? Here we need to look at both the numbers and the letters. Ask yourself 'what is the largest number and which common letter can be extracted?'

● the largest number that goes into both 3 and 6 is 3

● the algebraic term that goes into both xy and y^2 is y

So the biggest common factor to extract is $3y$. This gives

$$3xy + 6y^2 = 3y(? + ?)$$

Now ask yourself 'what do you need to multiply $3y$ by to

make $3xy$?' The answer must be x so the first term in the bracket is x

$$3xy + 6y^2 = 3y(x + ?)$$

Now ask yourself 'what do I multiply $3y$ by to generate $6y^2$? Now $2 \times 3 = 6$ and $y \times y = y^2$ so the term must be $2y$. So the answer is

$$3xy + 6y^2 = 3y(x + 2y).$$

You could check the answer by expanding the right-hand side and seeing if you get the same terms as on the left-hand side.

Example 3
Factorise $4x^2 + 5x$.

Here the numbers (the coefficients of x) do not have any common factors but the algebraic variables do. The common factor is x – there is an x^2 in the first term and an x in the second term, so we can extract an x from both

$$x(? + ?)$$

Again, what do we need to multiply x by to get the $4x^2$ term? The answer must be $4x^2$. So this is what it looks like at the moment

$$x(4x + ?)$$

Now we need to generate the $5x$ term – what do we need to multiply the x outside the bracket by to make $5x$? Clearly the answer is 5. So the final answer is

$$4x^2 + 5x = x(4x + 5).$$

Exercise 6.6
Complete the factorising of the following expressions – some have been started for you.

1    $8x + 6y = 2(4x + ?)$ 2 $9y + 12z = 3(? + 4z)$

3    $10x + 5y = 5(? + y)$ 4 $4a + 16b = 4(? + ?)$

5    $10x + 15y = (+   )$ 6 $9x - 27y = (   )$

7    $27x - 81y =$ 8 $30a - 25b =$

9    $6x^2 - 15x =$ 10 $7m^2 - 49m =$

Make a journal entry about factorising. Give examples that work with your notes and explain what you have done.

The difference of two squares

This is a special factorisation – one that relies on recognising when a term or a number is a square.

We discussed square numbers in Chapter 2. Remember, you get a square number when you multiply a number by itself. $1 \times 1 = 1$, so 1 is a square number; $2 \times 2 = 4$ so 4 is a square number.

In the same way, in algebraic terms can be square terms, for example x^2.

In mathematics the word 'difference' means subtract. So the point to remember about the technique called *the difference of two squares* is that it means we must first check if both terms are squares – then if there is a subtraction to do.

For example, in the expression $m^2 - 25$ both terms are squares *and* it is a subtraction – therefore it is a difference of two squares.

So how do we factorise a difference of two squares? Here is the rule

difference of two squares = $(\sqrt{1\text{st}} + \sqrt{2^{\text{nd}}})(\sqrt{1\text{st}} - \sqrt{2^{\text{nd}}})$

Remember, $\sqrt{}$ means 'the square root of'. So

$m^2 - 25 = (m + 5)(m - 5)$

Convince yourself by expanding the brackets on the right-hand side. This should take you back to the expression on the left-hand side.

Exercise 6.7
Factorise the following expressions using the difference of squares method.

1 $x^2 - y^2$

2 $t^2 - y^2$

3 $a^2 - b^2$

4 $a^2 - 1$

5 $9g^2 - h^2$

6 $16x^2 - y^2$

7 $x^2 - \dfrac{1}{4}$

8 $9a^2 - 16b^2$

9 $9y^2 - z^2$

10 $16a^2 - \dfrac{9}{25}b^2$

Pause and reflect now. Write a journal entry and say how you feel about factorising. You also need to make some clear notes about how to factorise expressions.

Squaring negatives
Squaring negative terms can cause confusion, but there is a simple rule to follow:

- multiplying two terms with signs that are the same gives a positive answer;

- multiplying two terms with signs that are different gives a negative answer.

So
$$+ \times + \rightarrow +$$
$$- \times - \rightarrow +$$
$$+ \times - \rightarrow -$$
$$- \times + \rightarrow -$$

How to factorise quadratic expressions

Quadratic expressions are those in which the highest power is 2. This means there is a squared term in there somewhere.

By definition, quadratic equations have two solutions. In Chapter 8 we will look at the graphs of quadratic equations and you will see the connection between the graph and what is given in this section. Until then, let's go through an introduction.

Investigating $a \times b = 0$

Think about a multiplication where the answer is zero – what does that tell you about the terms in the multiplication? Clearly one or both of these terms must be zero. Convince yourself of this fact and then convince another person.

Try 1×0 or 2×0 or anything times zero and you will always get zero. We will come back to use this fact when solving quadratics by factors.

Factorising quadratics

Remember a quadratic is an expression that is usually of the form $ax^2 + bx + c$. Here, a is a number *not* equal to zero and b and c are also numbers. Factorising means rewriting the expression as a product of two factors. Remember, factorisation it is the reverse process of expansion.

Getting started with this is largely a matter of trial and improvement initially, but with practice it will become easy to spot what is happening. However, you do need to be aware that not all quadratics can be factorised.

Quadratics with positive coefficients

First we are going to consider examples in which b and c are both positive numbers.

Example 1

This means we want to rewrite expressions such as $x^2 + 5x + 6$ in the form $(x + ?)(x + ?)$, where the question marks are replaced by whole numbers.

We can find these numbers by examining each of the coefficients (the numbers in front of the x's).

Coefficients of 1	Remember, when a coefficient is 1 we do not write the coefficient in front of the variable (letter). So when a variable is denoted as, say, x this means that there is only one x here. Where there is no coefficient in front of the variable, then it is taken to be 1.

The coefficient of x^2 in $x^2 + 5x + 6$ is 1. So the first step here is to check that the coefficient of x^2 in the product of $(x + ?)(x + ?)$ is also 1.

$$(x + ?)(x + ?)$$
$$x^2$$

The diagram shows that the coefficients do agree.

The *constant term* in the original expression is 6 and this gives a good clue about the two numbers that are going to replace the question marks in the factorisation above. It means that we need to look for factors of 6 – two numbers that multiply together to give 6. This means that we need to consider 1 and 6, and 3 and 2.

But we also need these numbers to add up to the coefficient of the x term in the expression, namely 5. This means the factors we choose must be 3 and 2. So the full factorisation is,

$$x^2 + 5x + 6 = (x + 3)(x + 2).$$

Check: expand the right-hand side of the equation and you should find it takes you back to the left-hand side.

This technique can be summarised as follows.

- Check the coefficient of x^2.

- Examine the constant term and consider possible factors.

- Choose the correct factors by comparing with the coefficient of x.

Example 2

$$x^2 + 5x + 4 = (? + ?)(? + ?)$$

- Checking the coefficient of x^2 shows it to be 1.

- The constant term is 4 which has factors of 2×2 and 1×4.

- The factors chosen should add up to make 5, the coefficient of x. So the factors must be 1 and 4.

This means that

$$x^2 + 5x + 4 = (x + 1)(x + 4).$$

Check: expand the right-hand side of the equation and you should find it takes you back to the left-hand side.

Exercise 6.8

Factorise these quadratic expressions.

1	$x^2 + 9x + 20$	2	$x^2 + 12x + 35$
3	$x^2 + 17x + 60$	4	$x^2 + 10x + 21$
5	$x^2 + 16x + 15$	6	$x^2 + 8x + 15$
7	$x^2 + 11x + 18$	8	$x^2 + 12x + 11$
9	$x^2 + 8x + 12$	10	$x^2 + 14x + 45$

This section on factorising quadratic expressions has shown that quadratics of the form $x^2 + bx + c$ can be factorised and that they take the form $(x + \times)(x + \times)$, where $\times$ and $\times$ are positive numbers.

Quadratics of the form $x^2 - bx + c$

Notice the difference here. Both signs were positive in the quadratic form above – here one sign is negative and that does have implications for what we do. Now we have to look at the sign of each term very carefully.

Example 1

Let's factorise $x^2 - 11x + 30$ so that it comes out in the form $(x + ?)(x + ?)$.

- First of all check the coefficient of x^2 – in this case it is 1 so that's OK so far.

- Look at the constant term – we need to find two numbers that multiply together to give +30. Possible combinations include +10 and +3, + 15 and +2, +1 and +30, and +5 and +6.

But there is a problem – we need to have a negative coefficient of x and none of these combinations will give us a negative $11x$. So we need to consider negative factors. The best way to tackle this is to consider two factors that multiply to give the constant but add to give the coefficient of x.

Think about this for a moment – what two numbers will multiply to +30 and add to –11? This implies that both must be negative (remember, a negative multiplied by a negative gives a positive; and a larger negative added to a smaller negative gives a negative).

The factors must be –6 and –5. So the factorisation is

$$x^2 - 11x + 30 = (x - 6)(x - 5).$$

Check: expand the brackets on the right-hand side and you should get the left-hand side. (Don't forget to tidy up the quadratic by adding the two middle terms.)

Look at how the quadratic has factorised. The –6 in the first bracket and the x in the second bracket have been multiplied together to give $-6x$ and the –5 and the other x have multiplied together to give $-5x$. In the same way the –6 and –5 have multiplied to generate the +30.

Example 2
Factorise $a^2 - 5a + 6$.

Here we want factors of +6 that add up to –5. The first step is to check the coefficient of a. This is 1 so we can confidently say that it will factorise in the form

$$a^2 - 5a + 6 = (a\ ?)(a\ ?)$$

No we list the possible factors that we can use here. Since we need to generate +6 as the constant term we know that the factors must both be either positive numbers or negative numbers. Try some now.

The possibilities are –1 and –6, or +1 and +6, or –2 and –3, or +2 and +3. We also need them to add to the coefficient of x, and that is –5. This means the factors we need must be –2 and –3. So the factorisation is

$$a^2 - 5a + 6 = (a - 2)(a - 3).$$

Don't forget to check this solution.

This section is on factorising quadratics of the form $x^2 - bx + c$ where a, b and c are positive whole numbers factorise into the form $(x - \alpha)(x + \beta)$, where α and β are both positive.

Quadratics with a negative constant term

This section refers to quadratics of the form $x^2 + bx - c$ and $x^2 - bx - c$. In other words quadratic expressions in which the constant term is negative and the coefficient of x may be positive or negative.

Example 1

Factorise $x^2 + x - 12$.

A factorisation of the form $(x + ?)\ (x + ?)$ will give an x^2 term with a coefficient of 1 *but* the constant term is –12 and that suggests that one of the missing numbers must be positive and one must be negative. Therefore we are looking for factors of –12 that add to +1.

Study tip	Think about this for a moment – remember the running theme in this book is first to convince yourself and then to convince another person.
	Use your journal to make an entry now. Express how you feel emotionally and assess your understanding of the process so far. Write down how well you are doing and don't be too hard on yourself.
	Now write down all of the factors of –12, and do make sure you have them *all*. Now look for the factors that add up to +1 and write them down.

Back to the factorisation. The factors of –12 are –1 and +12, or +1 and –12, or +3 and –4, or –3 and +4. We also need them to add to +1; so that means that we must use –3 and +4. So, the factorisation is

$$x^2 + x - 12 = (x - 3)(x + 4).$$

Don't forget to do the check.

Example 2
Factorise $x^2 - x - 6$.

The numerical value of the coefficient of x^2 is 1 and so we can aim for the form $(x \pm ?) (x \pm ?)$.

The constant term is –6 and the coefficient of x is –1, so we need to find factors of –6 that add up to –1. This means that the factors must be –3 and +2. Therefore

$$x^2 - x - 6 = (x + 2)(x - 3).$$

Again you need to convince yourself and then convince another person. Expand the brackets on the right-hand side and that should give you the expression on the left-hand side.

Exercise 6.9
Factorise these quadratic expressions.

1    $x^2 - x - 2$ 2 $x^2 - x - 12$

3	$x^2 + 2x - 15$	4	$x^2 + 7x + 12$
5	$x^2 + 5x - 14$	6	$x^2 + 2x - 35$
7	$x^2 + 7x - 18$	8	$x^2 - 16$
9	$x^2 + 11x - 12$	10	$x^2 + x - 90$

Changing the subject

This operation is also known as transposition of formulae or transformation of formulae. By *changing the subject*, we mean rearranging the equation to make any one of the variable letters appear on its own on one side of the equation by making sure that everything else is moved to the other side of the equal sign. To do this, you use exactly the same rules as when solving equations – in other words, you have the skills already.

Making *x* the subject

This means that we want to get x on its own on one side of the equation. So, for example, starting with, if we want x to be the subject, we need to get the x term on its own and everything else on the other side of the equal sign.

Example 1

Starting with $f = y + 3x$, the first thing to do is to take y from both sides

$$f - y = y + 3x - y$$

The y's on the right-hand side cancel each other out, so the next line looks like this

$$f - y = 3x$$

Now we need to undo the 3 times x on the right-hand side – this means by dividing both sides by 3

$$\frac{f - y}{3} = \frac{3x}{3}$$

Now the 3s on the right-hand side cancel leaving

$$x = \frac{f - y}{3}.$$

Example 2

Let's look at example involving brackets. We want to make x the subject in this equation

$$v(x + v) = y^2$$

First, expand the brackets

$$vx + v^2 = y^2$$

Now subtract v^2 from both sides

$$vx + v^2 - v^2 = y^2 - v^2$$
$$vx = y^2 - v^2$$

Now look at the left-hand side – this is a product, it is $v \times x$, so to make x the subject we undo this by dividing both sides by v. This gives

$$\frac{vx}{v} = \frac{y^2 - v^2}{v}$$
$$x = \frac{y^2 - v^2}{v}$$

because the v's on the left-hand side cancel.

Check: it could be a bit tricky checking this one by substitution in the original equation!

Dealing with fractions

A fraction is a quotient – in other words, one quantity is divided by another. So we can undo it by multiplying, in just the same way as you did with equations.

Suppose $\frac{m}{p} = y$.

If we want to make m the subject we need to undo the division in this fraction.

To do this you multiply both sides by whatever is in the denominator of the fraction, in this case p.

Have a go at this now, multiply both sides by p and don't forget to cancel on the left-hand side. Have a go at this before you look at our solution.

$$\cancel{p} \times \frac{m}{\cancel{p}} = p \times y$$

$$m = py.$$

Dealing with square roots

A square root is often in the denominator of a fraction. For example, $y = \dfrac{p}{\sqrt{x}}$. This can look a bit scary but don't panic.

Example 1

To make x the subject of this expression, remember that you can look to eliminating the fraction by multiplying both sides by a certain term. In this example, multiply both sides by $\sqrt{x}$. This will mean that the $\sqrt{x}$ term will cancel on the right-hand side

$$\sqrt{x} \times y = \sqrt{x} \times \frac{p}{\sqrt{x}}$$

So now we have $\sqrt{x}\,y = p$. This is better, but we want x on its own on one side of the equation and everything else on the other side.

Look at the left-hand side of the equation. There are two terms side by side – in algebra this means a product – so these two terms are multiplied together. If they are multiplied they can be divided and that is what we need to do next. We want x on its own and the closest we have is $\sqrt{x}\,y$ so therefore we divide both sides by y and this will leave the $\sqrt{x}$ on its own.

$$\frac{\sqrt{x}\,\cancel{x}}{\cancel{x}} = \frac{p}{y}$$

$$\sqrt{x} = \frac{p}{y}.$$

Now we are close to what we want – but we want x rather than $\sqrt{x}$ How do we get from $\sqrt{x}$ to x?

The simple answer is to square it because $\sqrt{x} \times \sqrt{x} = x$. But we must do the same thing to both sides of the equation so

$$\left(\sqrt{x}\right)^2 = \left(\frac{p}{y}\right)^2$$

$$x = \left(\frac{p}{y}\right)^2.$$

Example 2

Make x the subject of

$$v = \frac{m}{\sqrt{x}}.$$

Multiply both sides by $\sqrt{x}$ to eliminate the fraction. This gives

$$\sqrt{x}\,v = \frac{\sqrt{x}\,m}{\sqrt{x}}$$

Cancel the $\sqrt{x}$'s on the right-hand side to give

$$\sqrt{x}\,v = m$$

Again we have a product on the left-hand side, so to isolate the $\sqrt{x}$ we divide both sides by v

$$\frac{\sqrt{x}\,v}{v} = \frac{m}{v}$$

The v's on the left-hand side cancel leaving $\sqrt{x} = \dfrac{m}{v}$. Now square both sides

$$\left(\sqrt{x}\right)^2 = \left(\frac{m}{v}\right)^2$$

$$x = \left(\frac{m}{v}\right)^2.$$

Example 3

Here is an example involve negative terms. We want to make x the subject of $b = m - \dfrac{t}{\sqrt{x}}$.

All we do is 'undo' this in stages as before. First subtract m from both sides

$$b - m = m - \frac{t}{\sqrt{x}} - m$$

$$b - m = -\frac{t}{\sqrt{x}}$$

Now we can use a technique described earlier – multiplying throughout by -1. This gives

$$m - b = \frac{t}{\sqrt{x}}$$

This is a lot easier to deal with, we have already seen equations in this format. Multiply both sides by $\sqrt{x}$ to eliminate the $\sqrt{x}$ on the right-hand side to leave t on its own

$$\sqrt{x}(m - b) = \sqrt{x} \times \frac{t}{\sqrt{x}}$$

$$\sqrt{x}(m - b) = t$$

All we need to do now is resolve the left-hand side by recognising that it is a product. The reason for not expanding those brackets should now be clear – we can divide both sides by $(m - b)$ and that will leave us with the $\sqrt{x}$ on the left-hand side to deal with as the next stage.

$$\frac{\sqrt{x}(m - b)}{(m - b)} = \frac{t}{(m - b)}$$

We cancel the fraction on the left-hand side.

$$\sqrt{x} = \frac{t}{(m - b)}$$

Now we need to square both sides, to eliminate the square root.

$$x = \left(\frac{t}{m-b} \right)^2$$

Example 4

Make x the subject of $bx^2 - h = y^2$

$$bx^2 - h = y^2$$
$$bx^2 - h + h = y^2 + h$$
$$bx^2 = y^2 + h$$
$$\frac{bx^2}{b} = \frac{y^2 + h}{b}$$
$$x^2 = \frac{y^2 + h}{b}$$
$$x = \sqrt{\frac{y^2 + h}{b}}$$

Exercise 6.10

Make x the subject of these equations.

1 $x + y = a + b$ 2 $xv - l = k$

3 $hj - x = b$ 4 $\dfrac{n(b-v)}{x} = y$

5 $n(b - x) = h + d$ 6 $dx^2 - k = g^2$

7 $f(a + x) = y$ 8 $\dfrac{m(x+d)}{a} = h$

9 $d(a + 9x) = y$ 10 $mx + y = c$

How to deal with algebraic fractions

$$\frac{5x^3}{8x} \quad \text{and} \quad \frac{8(x+9)}{2x}$$

are examples of algebraic fractions. As we have already seen, fractions can be simplified by cancelling when, and only when, there is a common factor in the numerator and denominator.

In your journal explain what is meant by a common factor? Remember the recurrent theme of this book – convince yourself and then convince another person.

Look at this operation to get the feel for common factors. It is written it out in rather a long winded way so that you can see what is going on. With practice you will be able to do problems like this in one step.

$$\frac{4x^4}{12x} = \frac{4 \times x \times x \times x \times x \times x}{12 \times x}$$

$$= \frac{1 \times x \times x \times x}{12}$$

$$= \frac{x^3}{12}$$

Example 1

Simplify $\dfrac{9(x+4)}{3x}$.

First, look for common factors. Obviously 9 and 3 will cancel because they have common factors, so

$$\frac{9(x+4)}{3x} = \frac{3(x+4)}{x}$$

You cannot divide the x's in this example because x is not a common factor.

In your journal make notes about what we have done here. On the left-hand side of the page note down this example, and preferably one of your own as well. On the right-hand side of the page, describe the steps in the method for simplifying these types of questions.

Multiplying algebraic fractions

When multiplying algebraic fractions, look for and cancel any factor that is common to both the numerator and the denominator. Then, when it is not possible to cancel any further, multiply the remaining numerators and denominators.

For example, suppose we want to simplify $\dfrac{x^8}{y^2} \times \dfrac{x^4 y}{z} \times \dfrac{z^6}{x^3}$.

Cancel the x's first. x^8 and x^3 will cancel to give x^5 on the top. Then cancel the y and y^2 and then the z^6 and z in a similar way. This gives

$$\frac{x^8}{y^2} \times \frac{x^4 y}{z} \times \frac{z^6}{x^3} = \frac{x^5}{y} \times x^4 \times z^5$$
$$= \frac{x^9 z^5}{y}.$$

Dividing algebraic fractions

When you divide something by an algebraic fraction, it is the same as multiplying it by its reciprocal. Look what happens when we do it with numbers.

$5 \div \dfrac{1}{3}$ means 'how many thirds are there in 5?'

Clearly there are 15 thirds in 5, so $5 \div \dfrac{1}{3} = 15$.

But the reciprocal of $\dfrac{1}{3}$ is 3, so since $5 \times 3 = 15$ we could have got the same answer by multiplying by the reciprocal.

Reciprocals

The reciprocal of any number is the number that you multiply it by to get an answer of 1. The reciprocal of 3 is $\dfrac{1}{3}$. The reciprocal of $\dfrac{1}{25}$ is 25. The reciprocal of $\dfrac{2}{33}$ is $\dfrac{33}{2}$.

So when you are dividing by a fraction, it has the same result as multiplying by the reciprocal of the fraction. It is easy to get the reciprocal of a fraction – just invert it.

$$6x \div \frac{y}{z} = \frac{6x}{1} \times \frac{z}{y}$$
$$= \frac{6xz}{y}.$$

Adding and subtracting algebraic fractions

When you are dealing with fractions written in number form, you cannot add or subtract the fractions unless they have a common denominator. The same is true for algebraic fractions.

Example 1

Simplify $\dfrac{4x+1}{3} + \dfrac{3x-2}{2}$.

The denominators are 2 and 3, so the lowest common denominator is the lowest common multiple (LCM) of the denominators of the fractions – in this case 6.

So we need to multiply the first fraction (above and below) by 2 and the second fraction by 3. So

$$\frac{4x+1}{3} + \frac{3x-2}{2} = \frac{2(4x+1)}{6} + \frac{3(3x-2)}{6}$$
$$= \frac{8x+2}{6} + \frac{9x-6}{6}$$
$$= \frac{17x-4}{6}.$$

Example 2

Multiply the first by 2 and the second by 4

$$\frac{6x-3}{4} - \frac{x+7}{2} = \frac{6x-3}{4} - \frac{2(x+7)}{4}$$
$$= \frac{6x-3-2x-14}{4}$$
$$= \frac{4x-17}{4}$$

Cancelling has been left until the end

$$= \frac{4x}{4} - \frac{17}{4}$$
$$= x - 4.25$$

Tutorial

Progress questions

Expand these expressions.

1 $(x + 5)(x + 2)$ **2** $(x + 3)(x + 7)$

3 $(y + 2)(y + 4)$ **4** $(x - 4)(x + 5)$

5 $(2x + 2)(x - 4)$ **6** $(3x + 5)(x - 2)$

7 $(3d - 5)(4d - 7)$ **8** $(3f - 8)(4f + 2)$

9 $(7g - 4)(g - 3)$ **10** $(x + 7)^2$

11 $(f + 3)^2$ **12** $(x - 8)^2$

13 $(d + 2)^2$

Simplify the following.

14 $\dfrac{x^4 y^3}{z^5} \times \dfrac{xyz}{x^2}$ **15** $\dfrac{18pb^2}{6pb}$

Solving Simultaneous Equations

One-minute overview

Simultaneous equations are two or more equations that have to be solved at the same time, hence the name 'simultaneous'.

In this chapter you will learn to solve simultaneous equations with two unknowns by using:

■ the elimination method;
■ the substitution method.

Solving equations with two unknowns

Solving equations with two unknowns is something of a problem because, so far as we have seen, it is only possible to solve an equation with one unknown.

Think about what happens in real life – if you have two mystery whole numbers that add to 10 they could be 1 and 9, or 2 and 8, or 3 and 7, or 4 and 6, or 5 and 5.

So it is not possible to solve a *single* equation where there is more than one unknown because we simply have too many variables. If you have two or more variables then you need more equations linking them to get a solution.

A pair of simultaneous equations would be something like

$$2x + y = 5$$
$$x + 3y = 5.$$

At this stage we do not know the values of x and y (unless you have guessed). But the point to understand here is that the value of x is the same in both equations. Similarly the value of y is also the same. This allows us to use one of two methods to solve these equations – either elimination or substitution.

The elimination method

The idea here is to remove one of the variables. This will leave us with just one unknown. Let's look at an example.

Example 1

$$a + b = 7 \qquad \text{(equation 1)}$$
$$2a + b = 10 \qquad \text{(equation 2)}$$

Here we need to consider the coefficients of a and b. Can we eliminate either the a's or the b's ?

Look at what happens if we work out (equation 2 – equation 1)

$$2a - a = a$$
$$b - b = 0$$
$$10 - 7 = 3.$$

The b's are eliminated – there aren't any left. So we are left with $a = 3$. The next step is to substitute for a in one of the equations – equation 1 would be the simplest to use.

Equation 1 is $a + b = 7$. Since we know that $a = 3$, then we can say that $3 + b = 7$ which means that $b = 4$.

Check: substitute for a and b into equation 2 (the one we didn't use in the substitution of a). This gives $(2 \times 3) + 4 = 10$, just as it should. So we know we are correct.

Substitution	In soccer, substitution means taking a player off and putting a different player on.
	In algebra, it means taking a letter out and putting a number in. In this example we are taking out the a and putting in a 3.

Example 2

$$2x + y = 9 \qquad \text{(equation 1)}$$
$$x - y = 3 \qquad \text{(equation 2)}$$

Look at the coefficients – for the y's are + and – so if we add them we can eliminate the y's.

$$2x + x = 3x$$
$$y - y = 0$$
$$9 + 3 = 12$$

So $3x = 12$. We must now is solve for x. Dividing both sides by 3 gives

$$\frac{\cancel{3}x}{\cancel{3}} = \frac{12}{3}$$
$$x = 4.$$

The next step is to substitute for x into one of the original equations, say equation 1.

$$(2 \times 4) + y = 9$$

therefore $y = 1$.

Check: putting $x = 4$ and y into equation 2 we get $4 - 1 = 3$, and that's as it should be.

Exercise 7.1

Solve these simultaneous equations by using the elimination method.

1	$2x + y = 10$	2	$x + y = 8$
	$x + y = 7$		$2x + y = 13$
3	$3x + y = 7$	4	$3x + y = 31$
	$x + y = 3$		$2x + y = 24$
5	$x + y = 3$	6	$2a + b = 20$
	$3x + 2y = 7$		$a + b = 15$
7	$a - b = 6$	8	$a + 4b = 25$
	$a + b = 12$		$a + b = 7$
9	$2x = 4 + y$	10	$3m - n = 5$
	$6x = 10y - 2$		$m + n = 11$

Make a journal entry now. Explain how the elimination method works.

The substitution method

This is the second method for solving simultaneous equations. In the substitution method, we rewrite one of the equations in terms of the other variable in the equation.

Example 1

$$x + y = 5 \qquad \text{(equation 1)}$$
$$2x + y = 9 \qquad \text{(equation 2)}$$

The first step is to rearrange equation 2 to make y the subject. So equation 2 becomes

$$y = 9 - 2x$$

Now here is the new bit – we substitute this into equation 1 so this now reads

$$x + (9 - 2x) = 5$$

Now let's tidy up

$$-x + 9 = 5$$

and add x to both sides and subtract 5 from both sides

$$-x + 9 + x - 5 = 5 + x - 5$$
$$9 - 5 = x$$
$$x = 4.$$

Now we have found the value of x, we can substitute for x into equation 1 to find the value of y.

$$x + y = 5$$
$$4 + y = 5$$
$$y = 5 - 4$$
$$= 1.$$

Check: putting $x = 4$ and $y = 1$ in equation 2 gives $8 + 1 = 9$ as it should do.

Example 2

$$3a - 2b = 0 \qquad \text{(equation 1)}$$
$$2a + b = 7 \qquad \text{(equation 2)}$$

Here we are going to rearrange equation 2 to make b the subject. To do this we need to take $2a$ from both sides giving

$$b = 7 - 2a$$

Now we substitute for b into equation 1

$$3a - 2(7 - 2a) = 0$$

Note that all we have done here is to take out the b and replace it with $7 - 2a$. This gives an equation with only a as the variable.

collect like terms

add 14 to both sides

divide both sides by 7

$$3a - 2(7 - 2a) = 0$$
$$3a - 14 + 4a = 0$$
$$7a - 14 = 0$$
$$7a = 14$$
$$a = 2.$$

Now substitute for a into equation 1.

add 2b to both sides

divide both sides by 2

$$3a - 2b = 0$$
$$6 - 2b = 0$$
$$6 - 2b + 2b = 0 + 2b$$
$$6 = 2b$$
$$b = 3.$$

So $a = 2$ and $b = 3$

Check: substitute for a and b into equation 2 giving $(2 \times 2) + 3 = 7$ as it should do.

An extra skill

There is one more area to be aware of – and that is where you have to multiply an equation throughout.

Example 1

$$2y + 5z = 24 \qquad \text{(equation 1)}$$
$$4y + 3z = 20 \qquad \text{(equation 2)}$$

Look at this	If 4 + 3 = 7 and we multiply every term by 2 then we get 8 + 6 = 14. This shows that if you multiply everything in an equation by the same number, the equality is still true. Try multiplying everything by 3 – you get 12 + 9 = 21.
	Try some more for yourself and convince yourself that this is always true, then convince another person.

Back to our simultaneous equations $2y + 5z = 24$ and $4 + 3z = 20$.

Look at the coefficients of y and z. There is absolutely no point in adding or subtracting these equations – it will not eliminate either of the variables. But there is another way of dealing with the equations – look at equation 1.

$$2y + 5z = 24$$

If we double everything in this equation look what happens

$$4y + 10z = 48 \text{ (equation 3)}$$

We have generated a new equation to put with equation 2.

$$4y + 10z = 48 \qquad \text{(equation 3)}$$
$$4y + 3z = 20 \qquad \text{(equation 2)}$$

Now we have two coefficients that are the same so we can eliminate the y's and then carry on as before. You try it now and compare your solution with the one below.

You should get $y = 2$ and $z = 4$.

Exercise 7.2

Solve the following simultaneous equations.

1    $a + b = 9$ 2 $a + 2b = 8$

     $2a - 3b = 8$ $2a + 3b = 14$

3	$2m + n = 17$	4	$2x + 2y = 10$
	$5m + 2n = 40$		$x + 2y = 8$
5	$5r + 2s = 44$	6	$6x + 2y = 50$
	$2r - s = 5$		$3x + 2y = 29$
7	$a + 2b = 25$	8	$m + n = 9$
	$2a + b = 35$		$3m + 5n = 41$
9	$2a + 3b = 63$	10	$x - y = -1$
	$2a + b = 37$		$2x - y = 0$

Problems solved by simultaneous equations

There are some real problems that we can solve using simultaneous equations. They are the type of problem where we need to establish two equations.

Find two numbers whose sum is 18 and difference is 12. Let's call the numbers x and y.

$$x + y = 18 \qquad \text{(equation 1)}$$
$$x - y = 12 \qquad \text{(equation 2)}$$

Look at the coefficients of y, there is a $+1$ and a -1 so adding will eliminate them. So adding equations 1 and 2

$$x + x = 2x, \quad y + (-y) = 0 \text{ and } 18 + 12 = 30$$

So $2x = 30$ and therefore $x = 15$.

Now we substitute for x into equation 1 getting $15 + y = 18$ and so $y = 3$.

Don't forget the check.

Exercise 7.3

1 Find two numbers with a sum of 12 and a difference of 4.

2 Twice one number added to three times another number gives 41. One lot of the first number added to one lot of the second number is sixteen. Find both numbers.

3 Three times one number plus twice another number gives 22. When one lot of each number is added together the answer is 9. What are the numbers?

4 Twice one number plus three times another number gives twenty-six. When one lot of each of the numbers are added together the answer is 10. What are the numbers?

5 Three litres of water and two chocolate bars cost £1. 15. Two litres of water and three chocolate bars costs £1.10. Find the cost of one litre of water and of one chocolate bar.

6 Three adult fares and one child fare on a bus costs £2.40. Four adults and two children on the same trip costs £3.40. Find the cost for one adult and for one child for this trip.

7 Two adult train fares and two child train fares for a particular journey cost £58.80. One adult and three children costs £47.40. Find the cost for one adult.

8 In a furniture store three chairs and two stools cost £290. Four of the same chairs and three of the same stools costs £395. Find the cost of one chair and of one stool.

9 Five sodas and three ice creams cost £5.25 whereas one soda and one ice cream cost £1.25. Find the cost of an ice cream.

10 A baseball cap and a mobile phone cost £26.49 but two baseball caps and three phones cost £72.97. Find the cost of a phone.

Tutorial

Progress questions

1 $2x + y = 16$ **2** $x + y = 9$

     $x + y = 9$ $2x + y = 14$

3 $3x + y = 10$ **4** $3x + y = 41$

     $x + y = 4$ $2x + y = 29$

5 $x + y = 3$

     $3x + 2y = 8$

6 Find two numbers with a sum of 9 and a difference of 5.

7 Twice one number added to three times another number gives 66. One lot of the first number added to one lot of the second number gives twenty-seven. Find both numbers.

8 Three times one number plus twice another number gives 39. When one lot of each number is added together the answer is 17. What are the numbers?

9 Twice one number plus three times another number adds to twenty-nine. When one lot of each of the numbers are added together the answer is 13. What are the numbers?

10 Three adult fares and one child fare on a bus costs £3.15. Four adults and two children on the same trip costs £4.50. Find the cost of one adult and one child for this trip.

Discussion

Make a journal entry on the techniques used in this chapter. Discuss the problem-solving techniques with another person – please remember the theme of this book, first of all convince yourself then convince another person.

Graphs and Algebra

One-minute overview

Graphs can be used to illustrate algebraic expressions.

In this chapter you will learn about:
- straight line graphs and their equations;
- graphs of simultaneous linear equations;
- graphs of quadratics and cubics.

Straight line graphs

Here is an equation which generates an easy graph to get started with, $y = x + 1$. The first step is to make a table of values. To do this we allocate values to the variable x and work out what the corresponding values of y are.

x	1	2	3
y	2	3	4

So the points to be plotted are $(1, 2)$, $(2, 3)$ and $(3, 4)$ where the numbers indicates the (x, y) points on the graph 8.1

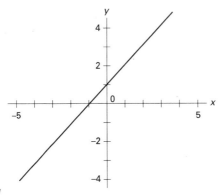

Graph 8.1

Notice we have only worked out three points. You can draw a straight line with just two points but the third is recommended for accuracy. So we have a graph that shows the equation of $y = x + 1$.

Look at the line on the graph. Choose a number on the x-axis (the horizontal one) and move up (or down) to the y-axis (the vertical one) – what do you notice?

Study tip

Make a journal entry now – explain how the graph was drawn and what you notice above

You should have noticed that at any point on the graph, the y-value is always one more than the x-value. Are you surprised by this? Think about the equation of the graph, $y = x + 1$. This equation tells us that whatever value of x you use, y will always be one more than it. This means that the equation of the line is the general rule that applies to every point on the line.

Let's look at another graph, $y = x + 2$. First we compose a table of values.

x	−2	−1	0	1
y	0	1	2	3

Now we can draw the graph. The points we plot are $(x, y) = (−2, 0), (−1, 1), (0, 2), (1, 3)$.

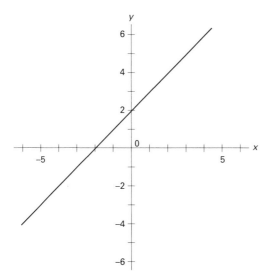

Graph 8.2

Look carefully at graph 8.2 and compare it with the graph of $y = x + 1$, what do you notice? You should see that it is essentially the same graph but it is shifted one up on the y-axis. In case you have problems seeing that, we have put them together in graph 8.3.

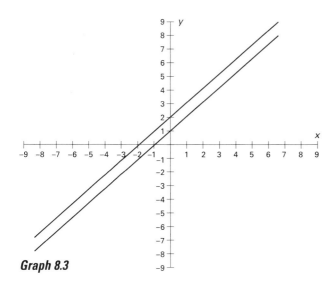

Graph 8.3

And so we can go on. In graph 8.4 we have added the line for $y = x$.

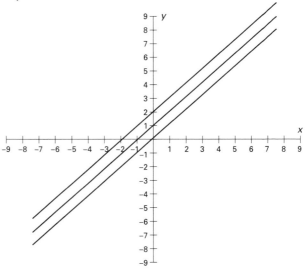

Graph 8.4

In graph 8.5 we have added $y = x - 1$.

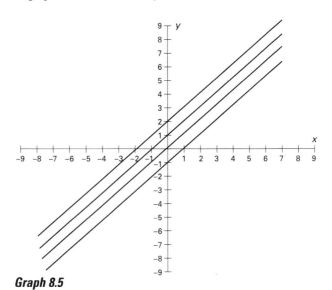

Graph 8.5

Make a journal entry now – explain what you notice about the graphs

You can see that:

● all these graphs are straight lines;

● all have the same slope – and are therefore the lines are parallel.

How do we work out the slope of a line?

The slope of a graph is called its gradient. The gradient is the 'drop divided by the step', in other words the distance along the *y*-axis divided by the distance across the *x*-axis.

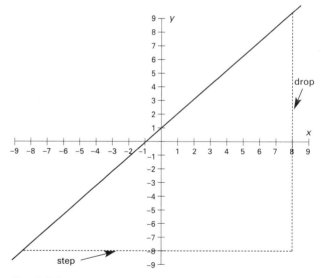

Graph 8.6

In graph 8.6 we have illustrated the 'drop' and the 'step' to make it clear what we mean. Mathematically, a drop is the difference between two *y*-values. In the graph in this example you calculate the drop shown with $9 - (-8)$; this gives 17.

Now do the same with the step shown here. This is the difference in the x-values. You should find that this also comes to 17 for this graph. (If you are not sure about these calculations, then simply count the squares.)

The gradient is conventionally represented by m. So in this graph of $y = x + 1$

$$m = \frac{\text{difference in } y}{\text{difference in } x}$$
$$= \frac{17}{17}$$
$$= 1.$$

So the gradient of this line is 1. Now work out the gradients of the other graphs we have drawn so far.

You should have found that the gradient of the line for all of the graphs is 1. This is a point we will come back to later. Now look at the equation of each line and the point where the line cuts through the y-axis, what do you notice here?

Look at the equations we have used so far:

$$y = x - 1$$
$$y = x$$
$$y = x + 1$$
$$y = x + 2$$

Now look at where each of their graph lines cuts the y-axis.

$y = x - 1$	cuts at -1
$y = x$	cuts at 0
$y = x + 1$	cuts at $+1$
$y = x + 2$	cuts at $+2$

and so on. So this gives us the idea that the last number in an equation, when it is written in this form, tells us where the line will cut the y-axis. But be warned, the equation might be written in a different form, as we shall see later in this chapter.

What about gradients?

Use the drop and step method to find the gradient of the line in graph 8.7.

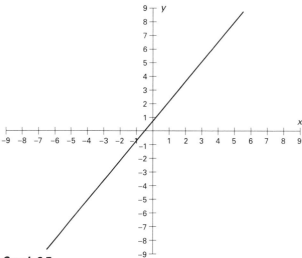

Graph 8.7

Now use graph 8.8.

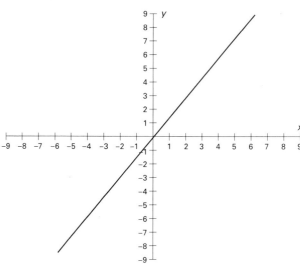

Graph 8.8

And finally graph 8.9.

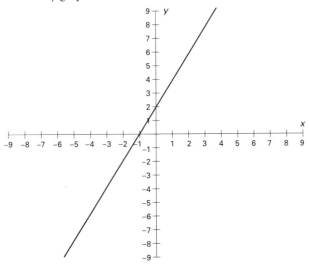

Graph 8.9

Now compare the gradients you have just calculated. Now compare the value with the coefficients of x in each of the equations. Write down what you notice.

Make a journal entry now – explain what you notice about the equation and the coefficients of x

You should have found that the gradients are the same as the coefficient of x in the relevant equation.

The form of the equation is important here, it tells us a great deal. The generalised equation of a straight line graph is written as $y = mx + c$

where m is the gradient of the line and c is the intercept on the y-axis (the point where the line crosses it).

This gives a shortcut to imagining what the graph will look like. Say, for example, we wanted to draw the graph of $y = 3x - 4$ we know straight way that it will have a gradient of $+3$ and will cut through the y-axis at -4. Let's look at the graph – it is shown in graph 8.10.

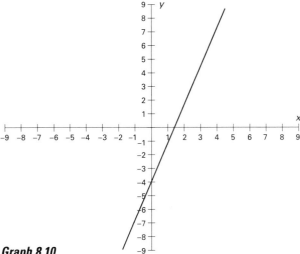

Graph 8.10

And you can see that this is exactly as we predicted. Notice what we have done here. We have gone from the particular to the general – we have found a *general rule* that applies to all equations that are written in this form.

Using this general rule $y = mx + c$ (sometimes written as $y = ax + b$), we can mentally see what the graph will look like. The value of m will tell you exactly what the gradient of the line will be and the value of c will tell you where it will cut the y-axis.

So $y = 6x + 3$ should have a gradient of 6 and cut the y-axis at +3. Graph 8.11 shows what it does look like.

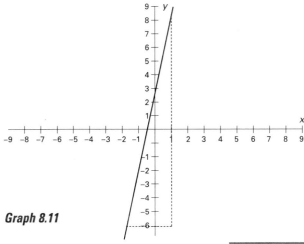

Graph 8.11

Writing equations in different forms

We mentioned above that equations can be written in different forms. Look at this example,

$x + y = 5$

This is a simple equation with two unknown variables. We can rearrange the equation to make y the subject (using the rules described in earlier chapters)

$y = 5 - x$

This is the form the equation should be in to draw its graph. Now let's get a table to give a set of coordinates to plot. We'll do this one step-by-step.

x	−1	0	1	2
y				

Notice what we have done – we have entered four values of x from −1 to 2.

constant	5	5	5	5
x	−1	0	1	2
y				

Here all we have done is place the equation constant 5 across the columns – this will help in doing the sums. Now we are ready to calculate the y values using the equation skills you learned in earlier chapters.

constant	5	5	5	5
x	−1	0	1	2
y	6	5	4	3

Graph 8.12 shows what the graph of $y = 5 - x$ looks like.

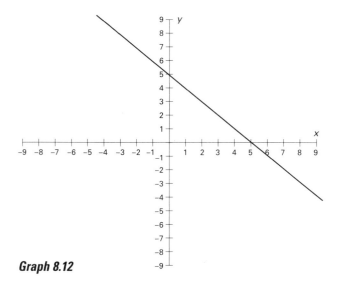

Graph 8.12

Notice the x term is negative in this equation – this indicates that the gradient is also negative.

So we have a set of rules for determining the nature of the graph of an equation:

- the constant (c) gives the intercept on the y-axis;

- if the coefficient of x is negative, the gradient is negative and must slope from top left to bottom right;

- if the coefficient of x is positive, the gradient is positive and must slope from bottom left to top right.

Example 1

Using the equation $y = 6 - 2x$, copy the table below into your journal and complete it.

constant	6	6	6	6	6
x	−1	0	1	2	3
2x	−2	0	2		
y		6	4		

Now draw the graph and you should find it looks like that shown in graph 8.13.

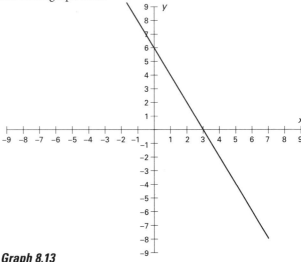

Graph 8.13

As we have said many times before, convince yourself and then convince another person.

Exercise 8.1
Draw the graphs of the following equations.

1	$y = x + 4$	**2**	$y = x - 3$
3	$y = x + 7$	**4**	$y = x - 9$
5	$y = 2x + 7$	**6**	$y = 2x + 3$
7	$y = 7x + 7$	**8**	$y = 3x + 2$
9	$y = 8 - 2x$	**10**	$y = 7 - 5x$

Straight line graphs and simultaneous equations

In Chapter 7 we looked at simultaneous equations and used two methods to solve them – both algebraic. We can also solve them graphically. Let's look at these two simultaneous equations and their graphs

$$\begin{matrix} x + y = 7 \\ 2x + y = 10 \end{matrix} \text{ which rearrange to } \begin{matrix} y = 7 - x \\ y = 10 - 2x \end{matrix}$$

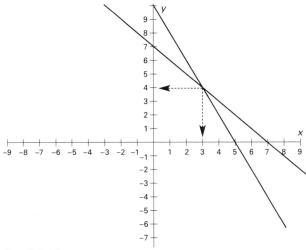

Graph 8.14

The lines in graph 8.14 represent points that satisfy each equation. Because these are simultaneous equations, there has to be a point where the values of x and y are the same on *both* lines. This point give the solutions to the simultaneous equations.

This must be where the lines cross. In other words, the point where the lines cross is the only point that satisfies both equations and therefore this must give the solutions. Here the solutions are $x = 3$, $y = 4$ and this is indicated on the diagram.

Example 1

Find the solutions to these simultaneous equations

$$y = 9 - 2x$$
$$y = x + 3.$$

Copy and complete the tables below.

First for $y = 9 - 2x$

constant	9	9	9	9	9
x	0	1	2	3	4
2x	0	2	4		
y	9	7			

Now for $y = x + 3$

constant	3	3	3	3	3
x	0	1	2	3	4
y	3	4			

Now draw the graphs and compare them with ours shown in graph 8.15.

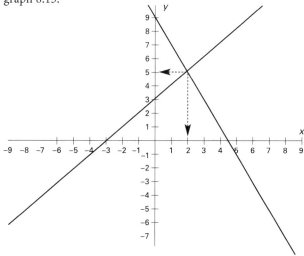

Graph 8.15

Again the values of x and y have been marked on the graph. So $x = 2$, $y = 5$ are the solutions to these equations.

Example 2

$$y = 10 - 2x$$
$$y = 7 - x.$$

Construct the table of values for each equation, first for $y = 10 - 2x$

constant	10	10	10	10	10
x	−2	−1	0	1	2
2x	−4	−2	0	2	4
y	14	12	10	8	6

and now for $y = 7 - x$

constant	7	7	7	7	7
x	−3	−1	0	4	6
y	10	8	7	3	1

The graphs look like as shown in graph 8.16 and the solutions are $x = 3$, $y = 4$.

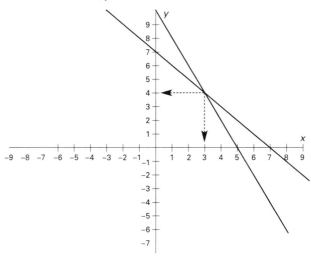

Graph 8.16

Exercise 8.2

Solve the following simultaneous equations by drawing graphs.

1   $y = 8 - x$
    $y = 13 - 2x$

2   $y = 7 - 3x$
    $y = 3 - x$

3   $y = 31 - 3x$
    $y = 24 - 2x$

4   $b = 3 - a$
    $2b = 7 - 3a$

5   $n = 20 - 2m$
    $n = 15 - m$

6   $y = 5 - x$
    $y = 2x + 2$

7   $y = 8 - 2z$
    $y = 6z - 16$

8   $y = 9x + 4$
    $y = 15x - 8$

9   $b = 7 - a$
    $b = 2a - 2$

10   $y = x + 1$
    $y = 10 - x$

Quadratic equation graphs

Remember, quadratic expressions are expressions where the highest power of x is 2. So it follows that a quadratic equation is an equation where the highest power is 2.

In this section we are going to look at how to draw quadratic graphs of the form $y = ax^2 + bx + c$.

Here is a simple example – graph 8.17 shows the curve for $y = x^2$. The equation is a curve – in fact it is called a parabola.

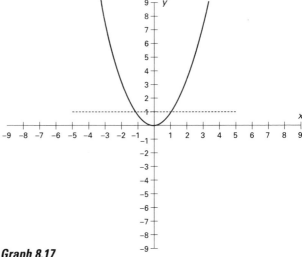

Graph 8.17

Look at what graph 8.17 shows. Every value of y on it is equal to the value of x after it has been squared. So when $y = 1$ we can read across to two points on the curve – at one of these points $x = 1$ and at the other $x = -1$.

Think about this for a moment, it makes a great deal of sense. Given that the equation is $y = x^2$, when $x = -1$ then $y = (-1) \times (-1)$ which is $= +1$. When $x = 1$ then $y = (+1) \times (+1)$ which again is $+1$.

So now you can see why quadratic equations have two solutions.

Investigating quadratic equation graphs

So let's investigate quadratic equations and their graphs now.

Example 1

We will use the equation $y = x^2 + 1$ as a starting point. As usual the first step is to construct a table of values.

constant	1	1	1	1
x	−1	0	1	2
2x	1	0	1	4
y	2	1	2	5

These (x, y) coordinates are plotted in graph 8.18.

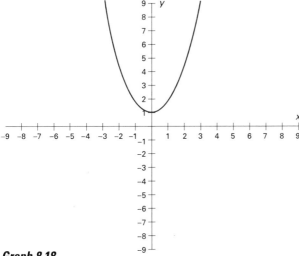

Graph 8.18

Compare this with the graph of $y = x^2$ (graph 8.17). What do you notice?

Study tip	Make a journal entry now – explain what you notice about the equation and the two quadratic graphs

What do you think the graph for $y = x^2 - 1$ will look like? Make a table of values, draw the graph and compare it with ours shown in graph 8.19.

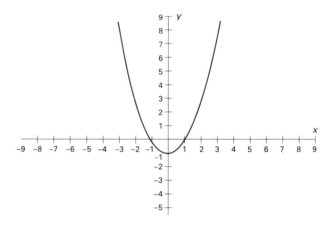

Graph 8.19

What about $y = x^2 - 2$? Maybe you can predict what it looks like now, without constructing a table and actually drawing it? Have a go at it and then compare your prediction with ours shown in graph 8.20.

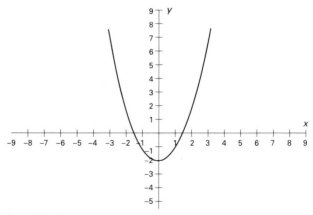

Graph 8.20

In graph 8.21 we have put all these $y = x^2 + b$ curves on the same axes, so that you can see what is happening.

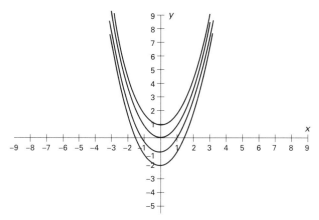

Graph 8.21

You can see that the constant in the equation moves the
turning point (the bottom of the curve) up or down the y-axis.

Example 2

What happens if we change the coefficient of x^2? Draw the
graphs of x^2 and $2x^2$ on the same piece of graph paper and
look at the similarities and differences in the graphs.

Study tip	Make a journal entry now – explain what you notice about the equation and the two quadratic graphs

Graph 8.22 shows our version – what do you notice?

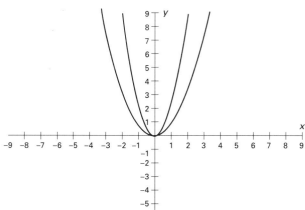

Graph 8.22

Graph 8.23 shows the curves of $y = x^2$ and $y = 5x^2$. As you can see, the larger the coefficient of x^2 then the narrower the curve becomes.

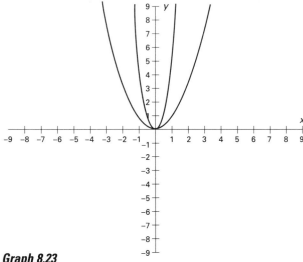

Graph 8.23

Example 3

This is a harder example, $y = x^2 + x$. First, we'll construct a table of values.

x	1	2	3	4
2x	1	4	9	16
y	2	6	12	20

Now we can draw the graph – it is shown in graph 8.24. Actually we have used more values than given in the table above – this is to show that the graph is symmetrical. You can check it by reading the values of x and y off the graph.

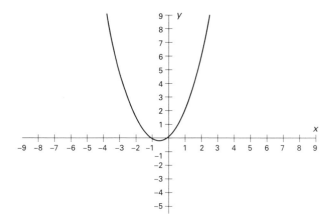

Graph 8.24

Exercise 8.3

Draw the graphs of the following equations using a scale of 2 cm for 1 unit on the *x*-axis and 1 cm for 1 unit on the *y*-axis. Use values of *x* from −10 to +10.

1	$y = x^2 + 5x$	2	$y = x^2 + 7x$
3	$y = x^2 - 4x$	4	$y = x^2 + 2x + 2$
5	$y = x^2 - 9$	6	$y = x^2 - 2x + 6$
7	$y = x^2 - 16$	8	$y = x^2 - 2x - 3$
9	$y = x^2 + 5x - 5$	10	$y = x^2 + 8x - 7$

What about quadratics with negative coefficients?

Draw the graph of $y = x^2$ and then draw the graph of $y = -x^2$. What do you notice?

> **Study tip**   **Make a journal entry now – explain what you notice about the equation and the two graphs**

Graph 8.25 shows the curve for $y = x^2$.

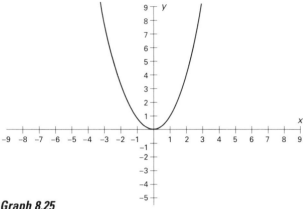

Graph 8.25

Now let's compare it with the graph of $y = -x^2$ shown in graph 8.26. You can see that it is a reflection of the curve for $y = x^2$ in the x-axis.

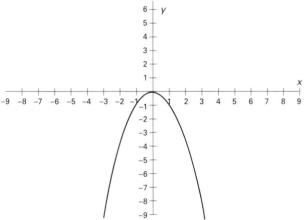

Graph 8.26

So from this we can deduce that when the x^2 term is negative, the curve is inverted.

What about cubic curves?

A cubic curve has an x^3 term as the highest power of x. Graph 8.27 is the curve of $y = x^3$.

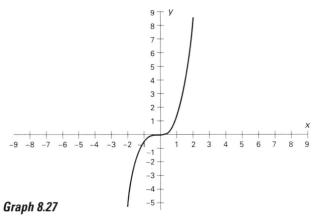

Graph 8.27

What happens as x gets larger? Here is one of those occasions which you really need to investigate for yourself – try different values for the coefficient of x. What happens another term is added? For example, $x^3 + 3$? Or $x^3 + x$? Or $4x^3 + 3x$.

Remember – you need to convince yourself first and then convince another person.

Example 1

Graph 8.28 shows the line for $y = 2x^3$.

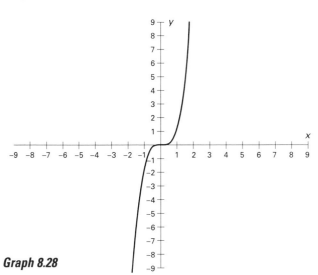

Graph 8.28

Graph 8.29 is the one for $y = 3x^3$.

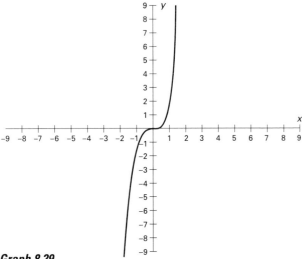

Graph 8.29

When you look at these three graphs individually there is little to separate them – but graph 8.30 shows what happens they are drawn on the same axes.

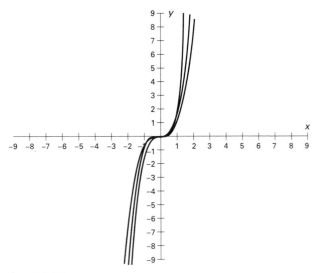

Graph 8.30

You can see that as the coefficient increases, the steepness of the curve also increases.

Example 2

At the start of this investigation we suggested that you draw the curve for $4x^3 + 3x$. Graph 8.31 shows what it looks like.

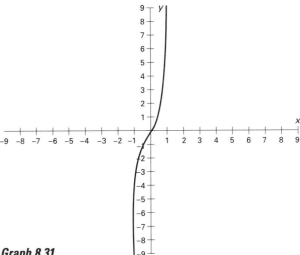

Graph 8.31

Example 3

The other type of cubic curve that you need to be aware of is shown in graph 8.32.

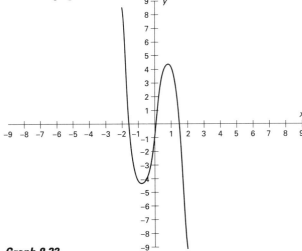

Graph 8.32

You can see in this graph there is a pronounced double turn. This is a common feature of cubic curves.

What happens when the x^3 term is negative?

Investigate this for yourself now. Make a table of values for $y = 8x - 4x^3$. Use values for x from –4 to +4 and plot the points on a graph. What do you notice about the curve?

Use your journal to make an entry to explain what you have done.

The two-stage process of convincing yourself and then convincing another person really does improve your understanding.

Graph 8.33 is for $y = 8x - 4x^3$.

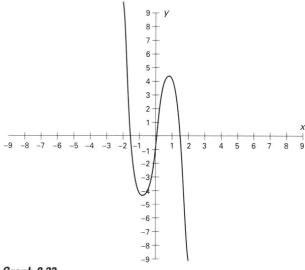

Graph 8.33

You should have worked out that as x gets larger, then so does y but y is negative.

Reciprocal curves

The final type of graph that you need to be aware of, in this chapter, is the reciprocal curve. These are derived from equations that include a fraction with an x term in its denominator – for example $y = \dfrac{11}{x}$.

Try a simple case, for example $y = \dfrac{1}{x}$.

Draw a sketch in your journal to show what you think this kind of curve looks like.

Example 1

Graph 8.34 shows the curves for $y = \dfrac{11}{x}$.

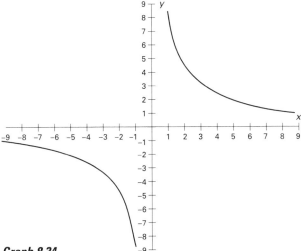

Graph 8.34

Notice that the curve has a break at $x = 0$. The x-axis and the y-axis are called *asymptotes* to the curve because the curve gets very close to but never actually touches the axes.

Example 2

Let's look more closely how we draw this type of graph using $y = \dfrac{10}{x}$ as an example.

First build a table of values.

x	−2	−1	0	1	2
10/x	10 ÷ −2	10 ÷ −1	10 ÷ 0	10 ÷ 1	10 ÷ 2
y	−5	−10	∞	10	5

The symbol '∞' means 'infinity' – a *big* number. Also note that you would need more points to draw this graph, but these will give you the idea. It turns out as shown in graph 8.35. Compare yours with this.

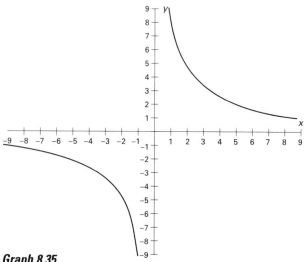

Graph 8.35

Example 3

Try this one on your own, $y = \dfrac{12}{x}$.

Make up a table of values and draw the graph. Graph 8.36 shows ours for you to compare yours against.

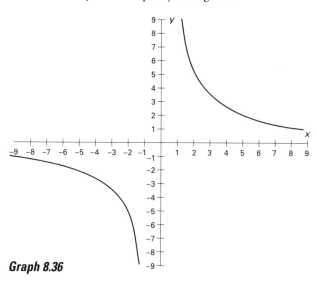

Graph 8.36

Example 4

The curves for $y = \dfrac{5}{x} + 6$ are shown in graph 8.37.

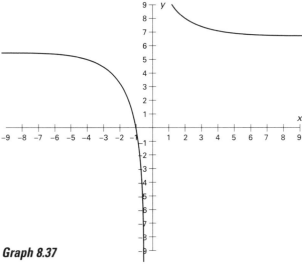

Graph 8.37

Tutorial

Discussion point

Drawing graphs of simultaneous equations is easier than using the algebraic methods to solve them.

Do you think this is true or false? Justify your view to another person. Make a journal entry.

Study tip

We recommend that you practice drawing the different graphs and use your journal to record the different methods. Try drawing a mind map for each method.

Solving Quadratic Equations

One-minute overview

Solving quadratic equations is a skill that will be useful throughout your mathematics career. In Chapters 7 and 8 you found that quadratics have two solutions and that this is clearly shown when a graph is drawn.

In this chapter you will learn about:
- factorising to solve equations;
- using of the formula;
- using the complete the square method as a way of factorising.

Remember to use your journal to keep a record of your work. We highly recommend this since it is a record of your *thinking*. All the members of the writing team used this approach when we were students, and we do find it really does work – and work well.

Earlier in the book we explained factorising. If you have skipped through some of the earlier sections, we recommend that you read and work through the section on factorising in Chapter 6 before starting this section. There will be a brief reminder here, but to gain the most benefit you need to feel comfortable with the work earlier in the book.

Factorising quadratic expressions: a reminder

Factorising a quadratic expression means to change its form so that it is in the form $(x + ?)(x + ?)$. When these brackets are multiplied out and all like terms are collected together, we should be back to the expression we started with.

Example 1

Factorise the expression $x^2 + 7x + 10$.

Think about the two terms that go where the ? marks are in $(x + ?)(x + ?)$. When these are multiplied together, they need to *multiply* to +10. This means that they have to be factors of +10. So they must be +5 and +2 or +1 and +10.

Now we need to decide which pair of factors works in this equation. The second condition to be satisfied is that these factors have to *add* to make the coefficient of the middle term. The middle term is $7x$ so the factors we need are +5 and +2.

So the final factorisation is $(x + 5)(x + 2)$. Try expanding this expression you should find that it takes you back to the original quadratic equation.

Example 2

Factorise the expression $x^2 + 3x - 18$.

Think through this yourself before you compare your answer with ours. You need to think in two stages – first of all what numbers multiply to give the constant? and then do they add to give the coefficient of the middle term?

We need to find factors of –18 that add to +3. They could be

+1 and –18
or –1 and +18
or +9 and –2
or –9 and +2
or +6 and –3
or –6 and +3.

Now, which of these pairs will add to +3? The only ones are +6 and –3, or –6 and +3. It doesn't matter here which you choose (but it might in later examples).

So, $x^2 + 3x - 18 = (x + 6)(x - 3)$ [or $x - 6)(x + 3)$]

Make a journal entry now – explain how we factorised the expression

Exercise 9.1

Factorise the following quadratic equations.

1	$x^2 + 8x + 12$	2	$x^2 + 8x + 15$
3	$x^2 + 12x + 20$	4	$x^2 + 20x + 36$
5	$x^2 + 12x + 35$	6	$y^2 - 7y + 6$
7	$a^2 - 11a - 12$	8	$b^2 - b - 20$
9	$x^2 - 2x + 24$	10	$y^2 - 16$

So how can we use this technique to solve equations?

The exercise above was about factorising expressions. These do not contain an equals sign – equations do.

You will always find that quadratic equations contain an x^2 term and usually an x term as well as a number term. Generally speaking, they have two solutions and there are three different methods to find those solutions.

Method 1: Solution by factors

Think about a multiplication in which two numbers are multiplied to give the answer zero. What does that say about one, or both, of the numbers multiplied? Make a note in your journal.

If you multiply two numbers and get zero then one, or both, of the numbers must be zero. Try some for yourself; 3×0, 5×0, 0×72, 3.2×0, ... It is one of these things that we instinctively know but find difficult to articulate. It is really useful in solving equations.

Example 1

The factors of $x^2 + 8x + 12$ are $(x + 6)(x + 2)$. So we can turn the equation

$x^2 + 8x + 12 = 0$

into $(x + 6)(x + 2) = 0$.

Now these two brackets are a product – and they multiply together to give zero. So one or both of them must be equal to zero. Therefore either $x + 6 = 0$ or $x + 2 = 0$. If $x + 6 = 0$ then $x = -6$. If $x + 2 = 0$ then $x = -2$.

These are the two solutions to the quadratic equation $x^2 + 8x + 12 = 0$.

Example2

$x^2 + 8x + 15 = 0$

Factorising gives

$(x + 3)(x + 5) = 0$

So either $x + 3 = 0$ and $x = -3$, or $x + 5 = 0$ and $x = -5$.

Study tip	Make a journal entry now – explain how these equations were solved

Exercise 9.2

Solve these quadratic equations.

1	$x^2 + 12x + 20 = 0$	2	$x^2 + 20x + 36 = 0$
3	$x^2 + 12x + 35 = 0$	4	$y^2 - 5y + 6 = 0$
5	$a^2 - 7a + 12 = 0$	6	$b^2 - b - 20 = 0$
7	$y^2 - 6y + 9 = 0$	8	$a^2 - 4a - 5 = 0$
9	$x^2 - 9x - 10 = 0$	10	$b^2 - b - 56 = 0$

What if there is no constant term?

Example 1

You can see that $x^2 - 5x = 0$ the left-hand side has two terms with a common factor, namely x. So we can take this out as a common factor to generate a new equation, $x(x - 5) = 0$.

We now have a product in which one (or both) factors must be zero. So either $x = 0$, or $x - 5 = 0$ when $x = +5$.

Equations such as this can be factorised by isolating a common factor first.

Example 2

$$x^2 + 7x = 0$$
$$x(x + 7) = 0.$$

So either $x = 0$ or $x + 7 = 0$ when $x = -7$.

Study tip	**Make a journal entry now – explain how this type of equation is solved**

Exercise 9.3

Solve these quadratic equations.

1   $x^2 - 4x = 0$ 　　　　　　 2 $x^2 + 8x = 0$

3   $2x^2 - 6x = 0$ 　　　　　 4 $x^2 - 25 = 0$

5   $6y^2 - 9y = 0$ 　　　　　 6 $25x^2 - 1 = 0$

7   $x^2 - 49 = 0$ 　　　　　　 8 $63x^2 - 21x = 0$

9   $4x^2 = 3x$ 　　　　　　　 10 $y^2 = y$

Method 2: Solution using the quadratic formula

Mathematics is a 'living' subject which is constantly developing – mathematicians are continually creating or discovering (depending on your viewpoint) new mathematics. This means it is legitimate, in our learning process, to make use of mathematics developed by previous mathematicians – in other words we do not need to discover everything for ourselves. There is a formula that can be used to solve a quadratic equation. Here it is and it is well worth memorising.

$$x = \frac{-b \pm \sqrt{(b^2 - 4ac)}}{2a}$$

This is a general formula that works on equations of the form $ax^2 + bx + c = 0$ where a and b and c are quantities, and where $a \neq 0$.

Example 1

Solve the equation $2x^2 + 3x - 5 = 0$. In this case $a = 2$, $b = 3$ and $c = -5$. So now we simply substitute these values in the quadratic formula. (Exam tip: in exams it really is worth stating the formula.)

$$x = \frac{-b \pm \sqrt{(b^2 - 4ac)}}{2a}$$

$$x = \frac{-3 \pm \sqrt{3^2 - (4 \times 2 \times -5)}}{4}$$

$$= \frac{-3 \pm \sqrt{9 - (-40)}}{4}$$

$$= \frac{-3 \pm \sqrt{9 + 40}}{4}$$

$$= \frac{-3 \pm 7}{4}$$

$$x = 1 \text{ or } -2.5$$

The standard practice in most mathematics courses is that you should use this formula *after* trying (and failing) to factorise. However, if you are *asked to factorise* in an examination but then use the formula, you will most likely not get the marks – even if you are correct.

Exercise 9.4

Solve these quadratic equations using the formula.

1	$2x^2 + 10x + 4 = 0$	2	$3x^2 + 11x + 5 = 0$
3	$6x^2 + 12x + 3 = 0$	4	$3x^2 - 11x + 2 = 0$
5	$5x^2 - 9x + 3 = 0$	6	$x^2 + 4x + 1 = 0$
7	$3a^2 - 2a - 5 = 0$	8	$3x^2 - 25x + 9 = 0$
9	$4x^2 - 5x - 4 = 0$	10	$9x^2 - 6x - 5 = 0$

Method 3: Solution using completing the square

We'll leave the actual solution for now and look at a method of factorising first.

Look at the equation $x^2 + 8x = 0$. We can call this equation a 'function of x' and write it as

$$f(x) = x^2 + 8x.$$

By writing this equation in the form $(x + p)^2 + q$ we are completing the square. This is a general rule and it applies when $p = \frac{1}{2}b$

(that's the b in the quadratic formula; 8 in this case) and $q = -p^2$.

Example 1

In $x^2 + 8x$, it can be seen that $p = (8 \div 2) = 4$.
Also $q = -p^2 = -(4^2) = -16$.

So $x^2 + 8x = (x + 4)^2 - 16$.

Prove this to yourself by expanding the bracket. Have a go at this now – expand $(x+4)^2$

$$\left(x+4\right)^2 = \left(x+4\right)\left(x+4\right)$$
$$= x^2 + 4x + 4x + 16$$
$$= x^2 + 8x + 16.$$

Can you see a problem with this? The +16 on the end shouldn't be there –that is why we use the final q term, remember $q = -p^2$.

Example 2

To factorise $x^2 + 6x$ it can be seen that $p = 3$ and $q = -9$. Therefore

$$x^2 + 6x = (x + 3)^2 - 9.$$

Again, prove it to yourself by expanding the brackets on the right-hand side and then adjusting the end number.

Example 3

To factorise $x^2 + 4x + 1$ we use the 'trick' of ignoring the 1 for a while and then putting it back.

So, $x^2 + 4x = (x + 2)^2 - 4$ by completing the square. Putting the 1 back we get $(x + 2)^2 - 4 + 1$, which simplifies to $(x + 2)^2 - 3$.

As always, prove it to yourself by expanding the bracket. Here

$$\begin{aligned}
(x+2)^2 - 3 &= (x+2)(x+2) - 3 \\
&= x^2 + 4x + 4 - 3 \\
&= x^2 + 4x + 1.
\end{aligned}$$

Example 4

Factorise $x^2 - 12x - 15$.

It can be seen that $p = 6$ and $q = -36$. So the expression we want is $(x - 6)^2 - 36 - 15$, or $(x - 6)^2 - 51$.

Prove this to yourself, then prove it to another person.

Example 5

This is a harder example – well it looks harder to start with, but we can simplify it to make it more straightforward.

Using $4z^2 - 16z + 7$ we need to take out the largest common factor – this is 4, so

$$4z^2 - 16z + 7 = 4\left[z^2 - 4z + \frac{7}{4}\right].$$

Now we can rework the right-hand side so that it is in the correct form to complete the square. Have a go at your producing your solution compare it with ours below.

Study tip

Make a journal entry now – explain how you used the completing the square method

Here is our solution.

$$\begin{aligned}
4z^2 - 16z + 7 &= 4\left[z^2 - 4z + \frac{7}{4}\right] \\
&= 4\left[\left(z-2\right)^2 - 4 + \frac{7}{4}\right] \\
&= 4\left[\left(z-2\right)^2 - \frac{9}{4}\right].
\end{aligned}$$

Using this to solve quadratic equations

Example 1

Solve the equation $x^2 - 8x + 6 = 0$ by completing the square. Remember, to complete the square the equation has to be in the form $(x + p)^2 + q$, where $p = \frac{1}{2}b$ and $q = -p^2$.

$$\begin{aligned}
x^2 - 8x + 6 &= \left(x-4\right)^2 - 16 + 6 \\
&= \left(x-4\right)^2 - 10.
\end{aligned}$$

From this we can create a new equation. Think about this for a moment, if

$$x^2 - 8x + 6 = 0 \text{ and}$$

$$x^2 - 8x + 6 = (x - 4)^2 - 10$$

then we can justifiably say that $(x-4)^2 - 10 = 0$. Now if we rearrange this equation we get

$(x-4)^2 = 10$.

Therefore,

$$x - 4 = +\sqrt{10} \quad \text{or} \quad -\sqrt{10}$$
$$x = \left(+\sqrt{10} + 4\right) \quad \text{or} \quad \left(-\sqrt{10} + 4\right)$$
$$= 7.16 \quad \text{or} \quad 0.86 \quad \text{(to two decimal places)}.$$

Example 2

Given that $f(x) = x^2 - 6x + 12$, show that $f(x) > 2$ for all values of x.

This looks intimidating at first but it doesn't need to be – first of all complete the square.

$$f(x) = (x-3)^2 + 12 - 9$$
$$= (x-3)^2 + 3.$$

Now $(x-3)^2$ is always greater than or equal to something squared because it is 'something squared' – it follows that $f(x) > 2$.

Study tip | **Make a journal entry now – explain how we used the completing the square method to solve quadratic equations**

Exercise 9.5

Complete the square for each of these expressions.

1   $x^2 + 6x$ 2 $x^2 - 10x$

3   $x^2 + 2x$ 4 $x^2 + 6x + 1$

5   $x^2 - 6x + 10$

Solve these equations by completing the square.

6   $x^2 + 6x - 3 = 0$ 7 $x^2 - 6x - 6 = 0$

8   $x^2 + 2x = 1$ 9 $x^2 + x = 1$

10   $x^2 - x - 1 = 0$

Tutorial

Progress questions

Factorise these quadratic equations.

1 $x^2 + 8x + 12$ **2** $x^2 + 9x + 18$

3 $x^2 + 14x + 24$ **4** $x^2 + 19x + 48$

Use the quadratic formula to solve these equations.

5 $2x^2 + 12x + 4 = 0$ **6** $4x^2 + 11x + 5 = 0$

7 $6x^2 + 9x + 3 = 0$ **8** $5x^2 - 11x + 2 = 0$

9 $x^2 + 6x = 0$ **10** $x^2 - 4x - 2 = 0$

11 $x^2 + 2x = 0$ **12** $x^2 + 6x + 1 = 0$

Discussion points

1 Write down a sequence of steps for completing the square. Explain how to complete the square to another person.

2 Make a journal entry on the work you have covered in this chapter. Make the methods clear in your notes. Write an example on the left-hand side and put notes on the right-hand side in a different colour. Explain the methods to another person, remember when the other person does not understand, your explanation has not been clear.

Bisections and Iterations

One-minute overview

We want to introduce you to a useful technique called *bisecting an interval*. However, to do this we need to take you through an investigation in which we search for the square root of 2. At the end of the investigation we will recap – as always, it is important that you work with us and try the activities as we progress.

In this chapter you will:
- search for the square root of two;
- use iteration to solve an equation.

The search for the square root of 2

We are going to concentrate on finding approximate solutions to equations such as

$$x^2 - 2 = 0$$
$$x^2 - 2x - 1 = 0$$
$$4x^2 - 14x + 49 = 0.$$

You must *not* use $\sqrt{}$ function on your calculator – the reasons will become clear as we work through the work, but please bear with us for now.

First of all we are going to look at $x^2 - 2 = 0$. Rearranging this equation gives $x^2 = 2$. This tells us that the solutions of this quadratic equation are the positive and negative roots of 2.

Activity 1
Using your calculator, calculate 1.41^2, and now 1.42^2, and then $1.41^2 - 2$, and finally $1.42^2 - 2$.

Look at the calculations you have just done – what does this tell you about $\sqrt{2}$? Explain your deductions to another person. As always, first convince yourself and then convince another person.

Study tip **Make a journal entry now – explain what you have done and the significance for $\sqrt{2}$. When, and only when, you have done this look at our notes below.**

It seems logical from, the calculations done above, to deduce that $\sqrt{2}$ lies somewhere between 1.41 and 1.42. Remember, we are looking for the solution to $x^2 - 2 = 0$ (or $x^2 = 2$) and clearly $\sqrt{2}$ is the solution we are looking for *but do not use the square root function on your calculator yet.*

Let's look at the graph of $y = x^2 - 2$ (graph 10.1) This may help you to understand what is going on.

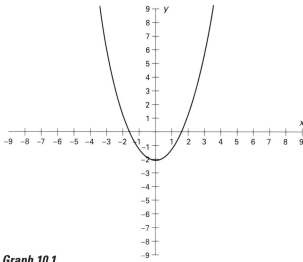

Graph 10.1

You need to be aware that whenever we talk about $\sqrt{2}$ it is taken that we mean the *positive* square root – but in this investigation we are interested in both roots as solutions to the equation.

Looking closely at the graph above shows us that the curve lies below the x-axis when $x = 1.41$ or -1.41, and above the axis when $x = 1.42$ or -1.42. Clearly, the graph crosses the x-axis somewhere between these points. It is at these points where the positive and negative square roots of 2 lie – in other words, $x = \sqrt{2}$ when the graph crosses the axis.

So all we have to do is find that spot and we will have found $\sqrt{2}$. Hmmmm! Let's take a step back.

Activity 2

• How did we determine the values 1.41 and 1.42?

• Calculate $1^2 - 2$.

• Now calculate $2^2 - 2$.

From this we can see that $\sqrt{2}$ must lie between the consecutive numbers 1 and 2 – simply because $1^2 = 1$ and $2^2 = 4$.

In mathematics we use specific names for certain ideas. When we have a range of numbers between two given numbers we call it an *interval*. So in the example above, we can confidently say that $\sqrt{2}$ lies in the interval between 1 and 2. But there has to be an easier way of saying 'the interval between …' – and there is, as we show below.

There is a standard notation which is used for intervals. In the case of the interval between 1 and 2, we write it as $[1, 2]$. This refers to all the numbers between 1 and 2 and *includes* 1 and 2. So we know that

$\sqrt{2}$ lies in this interval . There is a symbol which is used to indicate 'lies in this interval' or 'belongs to this interval'. It is $\in$. So we write the square root of 2 lies in the interval 1 and 2 like this

$$\sqrt{2} \in [1, 2]$$

This reads as 'the square root of 2 belongs to the interval one, two'. Now let's go back to the search for $\sqrt{2}$.

We know that the solution we require lies somewhere between 1 and 2.

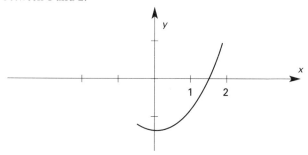

We can see from a graph like this that the curve crosses somewhere between $x = 1$ and $x = 2$, but we need to narrow this down.

This means that either that $\sqrt{2}$ lies between 1 and 1.5, or in our new terminology [1, 1.5], or it lies between 1.5 and 2, or [1.5 ,2].

How will we make this determination? How can we find whether $\sqrt{2}$ is in [1, 1.5] or [1.5, 2]? Discuss your ideas with another person, remember convince yourself and then convince another person.

Make a journal entry now – explain how to answer this question

The way to determine in which interval $\sqrt{2}$ lies is to do some simple calculations. If we calculate 1^2 and then 1.5^2 what will the answers tell us? We already know that $1^2 = 1$ so if 1.5^2 is greater than 2 we know that $\sqrt{2}$ must lie between these two numbers. If 1.5^2 is less than 2 then it must mean that $\sqrt{2}$ lies between 1.5 and 2.

Activity 3

Calculate the value of 1.5^2. Make a journal entry about what this tells you about $\sqrt{2}$.

Now $1.5^2 = 2.25$, so we now know that $\sqrt{2} \in [1, 1.5]$. Make sure that you know how we can be certain of this. If the square of the first element in an interval is too small (less than 2 in this example) and the square of the second element is too large (more than 2 in this example) then the solution we are looking for must lie in this interval.

The technique we have been using is called *bisecting the interval* and with it we can home in closer and closer on the required solution. This is an excellent technique for finding approximate solutions to equations.

The next step is to bisect the *next* interval. Think about what we are doing here – to start with we had a large interval

and we had to decide if $\sqrt{2}$ lay in $[1, 1.5]$ or in $[1.5, 2]$ – as we have mentioned above, it must lie in $[1, 1.5]$.

So we can draw a new diagram of our interval

Clearly we need to decide if $\sqrt{2}$ lies in $[1, 1.25]$ or in $[1.25, 1.5]$

Study tip	Make a journal entry now – explain how to answer this question

Again, some simple calculations will show which interval the solution lies in. We already know that the solution cannot be 1 since $1^2 = 1$, but could the solution be 1.25?
$1.25^2 = 1.5625$. So this tells us that 1.25 is too small to be

the solution. So this means the solution lies between 1.25 and 1.5. So we can say that $\sqrt{2} \in [1.25, 1.5]$

Here it is diagrammatically, and again we show the midpoint of the new interval

Now we have to decide if the solution lies between 1.25 and 1.375, or between 1.375 and 1.5. If we examine the mid-point we can determine whether the solution lies between 1.25 and 1.375 or between 1.375 and 1.5.

Make a journal entry now – explain how to answer this question

We square 1.375 and if the answer is less than 2, then $\sqrt{2}$ must lie between 1.375 and 1.5, but if the answer is greater than 2 then $\sqrt{2}$ must lie between 1.25 and 1.375. Calculate the value of 1.375^2 and decide which interval $\sqrt{2}$ lies in. Again convince yourself and convince another person.

Notice what we are doing here. We are following a certain set of instructions and *repeating* them as we head closer and closer to the solution. We can show this as a flow chart in which we follow some instructions and, depending on the answer, we modify the approximation to the solution and try again. Repeating the instruction is called *iteration*. Diagrammatically this process looks like

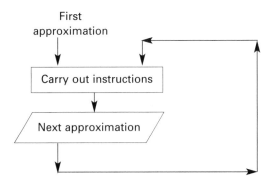

After one iteration we get the second approximation, after two iterations we get the third approximation and so the process continues. Continuing our example above, $1.375^2 = 1.890625$. This means that $\sqrt{2}$ must lie between 1.375 and 1.5.

Again we bisect the interval and select a new smaller interval.

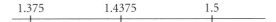

The midpoint in this interval is 1.4375 and again we have to decide if $\sqrt{2}$ lies between 1.375 and 1.4375 or between 1.4375 and 1.5. So we work out the value of 1.4375^2 and find that it is 2.06640625.

So because 1.4375^2 is greater than 2, it must mean that $\sqrt{2}$ lies between 1.375 and 1.4375.

Notice also that we must be pretty close to the value of $\sqrt{2}$ because 2.06640625 is pretty close to 2. So is $\sqrt{2}$ is going to be very close to 1.4.

Again we need a new interval to bisect,

You know the routine by now – take the midpoint, square it and use this as an indication as to which half of the interval the solution lines in. $1.40625^2 = 1.977539063$. The next interval to examine is [1.40625, 1.4375] but before we do that have a look at the diagram below. By engaging in subsequent iterations we are homing in closer and closer to the value of $\sqrt{2}$.

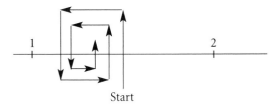

Start

Here is the next interval

1.40625   1.421875   1.4375

Once again work out the square of the midpoint, $1.421875^2 = 2.021728516$.

And this is where we are going to leave it because even though we don't have an accurate solution to $\sqrt{2}$ we have one that is pretty close ($2.021728516 \approx 2$).

The truth is that it not possible to determine the value of $\sqrt{2}$ exactly. We can get closer and closer but iteration will never give an exact determination because $\sqrt{2}$ is an *irrational number*. Such numbers fascinated the Greek early mathematicians simply *because* they could not be determined. This is why we asked you, at the start of this chapter, to avoid using the square root function on your calculator. Electronic calculators are programmed to approximate to $\sqrt{2}$ somewhere in the region of 1.414213562.

However we have used this investigation as a means of showing you the method of bisecting intervals to find the solution to an equation.

The bisection method

The way we found $\sqrt{2}$ was to use an ever decreasing series of intervals to home in on the value. After each iteration we chose either the left-hand or right-hand side of the interval to point to the direction to continue.

We need a way of showing this series of calculations mathematically. The way it is done it is to use *suffix notation*. The first calculation would be labelled x_1, the next x_2, then x_3, and so on. When we need to refer to an approximation without committing to a particular number we use the suffix n, so x_n reads as the nth approximation.

We also use this suffix notation for intervals. It seems that it is traditional to use early letters from the alphabet for the ends of intervals. So when we have a sequence of intervals we can refer to them as

$$[a_1, b_1], [a_2, b_2], [a_3, b_3], \ldots$$

When we searched for $\sqrt{2}$ we began with the interval $[1, 2]$ with the first approximation 1.5, which was clearly the midpoint of the interval. Mathematically this is written as

$$x_1 \in [a_1, b_1]$$
$$x_1 = \frac{1}{2}(a_1 + b_1) \text{ where } a_1 = 1, b_1 = 2 \text{ and } x_1 = 1.5$$

When we calculated $a_1{}^2$ we found it was less than 2, and when we calculated $x_1{}^2$ we found it was greater than 2; this led us to the conclusion that $\sqrt{2}$ lay in the interval $[1, 1.5]$.

We then used the second interval to calculate x_2. For the interval $[a_2, b_2]$,

$$x_2 = \frac{1}{2}(a_2 + b_2)$$

When we calculated $x_2{}^2$ we found that $x_2{}^2 < 2$ and that told us that $\sqrt{2}$ must lie between 1.25 and 1.5, in other words, $x_3 \in [1.25, 1.5]$. So in the third interval $[a_3, b_3]$

$$x_3 = \frac{1}{2}(a_3 + b_3) = 1.375.$$

And so on. It might be easier to see all this in a table.

n	a_n	b_n	x_n	$x_n{}^2 \geq 2$?	x_n replaces
1	1	1	1.5	yes	b_n
2	1	1.5	1.25	no	a_n
3	1.25	1.5	1.375	no	a_n

It is worth remembering that these values are approximate solutions to the equation. So how far out are they? The amount they are 'out from' the real answer is called the *maximum possible error*.

If we go back and look at the first iteration where we generated $x_2, x_1 \in [a_1, b_1]$ and

$$x_1 = \frac{1}{2}(a_1 + b_1), \text{ where } a_1 = 1, b_1 = 2 \text{ and } x_1 = 1.5.$$

We took the value of x_1 as the midpoint of the interval.

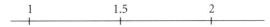

By taking the midpoint we are assuming it *will* be a solution to the value of $\sqrt{2}$. Since this is the midpoint of $[1, 2]$ the maximum error is 0.5, in other words in this interval the most we can be out from the true value of $\sqrt{2}$ is 0.5.

In the second iteration $x_2 \in [a_2, b_2]$ and

$$x_2 = \frac{1}{2}(a_2 + b_2)$$

and the maximum error is 0.25 ... and so on.

As you can see, the more iterations we do the closer we home in on the required value – that of $\sqrt{2}$ – so clearly maximum possible error decreases with the number of iterations,

It doesn't take much to see that the bisection method is a one we can use to solve more difficult equations of the form

(something in x) = 0

This method works when the value of the expression is negative on the left-hand side of the starting interval and positive on the right-hand side of the same interval.

Study tip	**Make a journal entry now – explain how this method works**

Using the bisection method to solve other equations

While there is a formula for solving cubic equations, it is both demanding and difficult to remember. Therefore we will use the bisection method. It is worth remembering that the method is a simple, ideal and reliable way of finding numerical solutions to equations.

Activity 4

We will solve the cubic equation $x^3 - 3x^2 + 4x - 5$.

The first step is to find an interval where the expression has different signs at the ends.

x	$x^3 - 3x^2 + 4x - 5$
0	–5
1	–3
2	–1
3	+7

From this we can see that since the sign changes between $x = 2$ and $x = 3$ we can conclude that this is the interval where the solution of the equation lies.

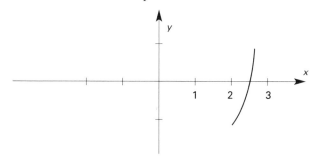

So we need to start bisecting intervals in order to determine an approximate solution that is less than 0.1 away from the actual answer – that is, within one decimal place of the final answer.

n	a_n	b_n	x_n	$x^3 - 3x^2 + 4x - 5 > 0$?	x_n replaces
1	2	3	2.5	yes (1.875)	b_n
2	2	2.5	2.25	yes (0.203125)	b_n
3	2	2.25	2.125	no (−0.451171875)	a_n
4	2.125	2.25	2.1875	no (−0.137939453)	a_n
5	2.1875	2.25	2.21875	yes (0.029022)	

Therefore, since 2.21875 is less than 0.1 away from the actual answer we can accept this as a solution to the equation *in the interval* [2, 3]. This is a cubic equation and therefore has three solutions – we have found only one of them. There are other intervals where solutions lie – but we will not be seeking them here! Graph 10.2 shows the curve.

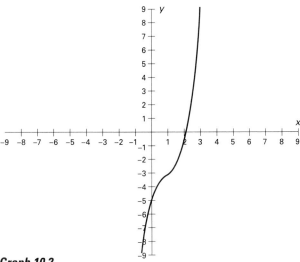

Graph 10.2

Tutorial

Progress questions

Use the bisection method to solve these equations.

1 $x^2 - 18x + 49 = 0$

2 $x^3 + 3x + 3 = 0$

Discussion point

Explain the bisection of intervals technique to another person. Go through each of the steps logically and make sure they understand why you are doing what you are doing.

Study tip

We recommend that you use your journal along with a set of mind maps. If you are new to mind mapping read Tony Buzan's excellent book *The Mind Map* (BBC books).

Answers to Exercises

Chapter 2

Exercise 2.1

Square number	1	4	9	16	25	36	49	64
Square root	1	2	3	4	5	6	7	8

Square number	81	100	121	144	169	196	225
Square root	9	10	11	12	13	14	15

Exercise 2.2

1, 8, 27, 64, 125

Exercise 2.3

1 $5s = e$ 2 $3s + 1 = e$

3 $10s + 1 = e$ 4 $2s + 3 = e$

5 $3s + 1 = e$

Tutorial: Progress questions

1   1, 4, 9, 16

2   a 10   b 12   c 20

3   1, 8, 27, 64

4   169

5   27

Chapter 3

Exercise 3.1

1   −1   2   −8   3   −8

4   1   5   +2   6   −5

7   −7   8   −7   9   −59

10 −16

Exercise 3.2

1	$4^2 = 16$	2	$5^3 = 125$	3	$4^3 = 64$
4	$9^2 = 81$	5	$7^4 = 2401$	6	$12^2 = 144$
7	$3^4 = 81$	8	$13^2 = 169$	9	$14^2 = 196$
10	$15^2 = 225$				

Exercise 3.3

1	w^3	2	m^7	3	j^{13}
4	a^8	5	g^{11}	6	r^2
7	e^5	8	d^6	9	s^{11}
10	y^4				

Exercise 3.4

1	p^6	2	j^3	3	r^3
4	w	5	q^6	6	a^3
7	m^6	8	h	9	y^2
10	n^6				

Tutorial: Progress questions

Set A

1	-2	2	-10	3	-6
4	-5	5	-2	6	$4^2 = 16$
7	$5^3 = 125$	8	$4^3 = 64$	9	$9^2 = 81$
10	$7^4 = 2401$				

Set B

1	w^4	2	m^8	3	j^{15}
4	a^{10}	5	g^{12}	6	x^6
7	b^3	8	c^2	9	y^{-7}
10	a^{-2}				

Set C

1	p^7	2	j^2	3	r^4
4	w^2	5	q^5	6	k^6
7	m	8	b^{-13}	9	n^5
10	a^{-10}				

Chapter 4

Investigation 1: Matchstick squares

$3s + 1 = m$ (s = squares, m = matches)

Investigation 2: Houses

$5h + 1 = m$ (h = houses, m = matches)

Investigation 3: Fishponds

$2f + 6 = s$ (f = fish, s = slabs)

Investigation 4: Ells

$2s + 1 = t$ (s = shapes, t = total)

Investigation 5: Frogs

$m = n^2 + 2n$ (m = moves, n = number of frogs on one side)

Tutorial: Progress questions

1   Where the highest power is one.

2   Where the highest power is two.

3   Where the highest power is three.

4   Calculate the differences and use this as an indicator of what you need to multiply by. This method works with linear relationships when the first differences are all the same.

5   As for answer **4** but then work out the second differences, which should be a power of 2 to show that the relationship is quadratic.

Chapter 5

Exercise 5.1

1	$z = 5$	2	$y = 11$	3	$v = 7$
4	$m = 3$	5	$f = 4$	6	$d = 20$
7	$a = 12$	8	$r = 28$	9	$a = 99$
10	$p = 81$				

Exercise 5.2

1	$x = 37$	2	$v = 27$	3	$c = 15$
4	$m = 47$	5	$k = 55$	6	$a = 20$
7	$l = 54$	8	$d = 110$	9	$q = 190$
10	$n = 275$	11	$k = 2$	12	$f = -6$

13 $k = -9$ **14** $h = 2$ **15** $f = -1$

Exercise 5.3

1 $y = 6$ **2** $m = 6$ **3** $n = 2$

4 $y = 3$ **5** $y = 2$ **6** $t = 12$

7 $u = 5.5$ **8** $r = 1$ **9** $f = 2$

10 $d = 4$

Exercise 5.4

1 $x = 27$ **2** $m = 40$ **3** $t = 21$

4 $y = 48$ **5** $t = 60$ **6** $a = 4$

7 $y = 6$ **8** $p = 33$ **9** $y = 90$

10 $k = 10$

Exercise 5.5

1 $x = 2$ **2** $x = 2$ **3** $f = 9$

4 $x = 6$ **5** $r = 7$ **6** $t = 1$

7 $p = 9$ **8** $r = 2$ **9** $y = 8$

10 $r = 6$

Exercise 5.6

1 $x = 2$ **2** $x = 9$ **3** $f = 7$

4 $x = 7$ **5** $r = 6$ **6** $t = 1$

7 $p = 2$ **8** $r = 3$ **9** $y = 10$

10 $r = 9$

Exercise 5.7

1 $x = 5$ **2** $y = 2$ **3** $t = 4$

4 $a = 9$ **5** $y = 7$

Exercise 5.8

1 $8c + 48$ **2** $2a + 6$ **3** $6t + 30$

4 $5u - 40$ **5** $3r - 27$ **6** $6y - 42$

7 $4y - 20$ **8** $6t - 18$ **9** $35y - 30$

10 $49t + 49$

Tutorial: Progress questions

1 $k = 3$ **2** $y = 10$ **3** $v = 13$

4 $m = 4$ **5** $f = 5$ **6** $x = 20$

7 $v = 26$ **8** $c = 17$ **9** $m = 48$

10 $k = 56$	11 $y = 7$	12 $m = 5$
13 $n = 6$	14 $y = 3$	15 $y = 2$
16 $x = 27$	17 $m = 40$	18 $t = 21$
19 $y = 48$	20 $t = 60$	21 $c = -3.25$
22 $a = 6$	23 $t = 3.5$	24 $u = 19$
25 $r = 18$		

Chapter 6

Exercise 6.1

1 $x^2 + 5x + 6$	2 $x^2 + 6x + 6$
3 $y^2 + 7y + 12$	4 $x^2 + 3x - 10$
5 $x^2 + 2x - 15$	6 $m^2 + 4m - 21$
7 $v^2 + v - 12$	8 $z^2 - 15z + 56$
9 $a^2 - 12a + 35$	10 $d^2 + 13d + 42$

Exercise 6.2

1 $2x^2 - 7x - 4$	2 $3x^2 + x - 4$
3 $12d^2 - 25d + 12$	4 $12f^2 - 2f - 30$
5 $7g^2 - 47g + 30$	6 $x^2 - 10x + 24$
7 $y^2 - 13y + 42$	8 $t^3 + 9t^2 + 4t + 36$
9 $-2y^2 + 16y + 168$	10 $60y^2 + 3y - 36$

Exercise 6.3

1 $x^2 + 8x + 16$	2 $f^2 + 10f + 25$
3 $x^2 - 6x + 9$	4 $d^2 + 14d + 49$
5 $m^2 + 4m + 4$	6 $g^2 - 6g + 9$
7 $2x^2 - 2x + 5$	8 $2k^2 + 28k + 100$
9 $2y^2 + 4y + 52$	10 $10x^2 - 20x + 20$

Exercise 6.4

1 $x^2 + 6x + 9$	2 $x^2 + 2x + 1$
3 $x^2 - 10x + 25$	4 $9x^2 + 12x + 4$
5 $16y^2 + 8y + 1$	6 $4x^2 + 48x + 144$
7 $2x^2 + 4x + 2$	8 $6x^2 + 36x + 54$
9 $5x^2 + 20x + 20$	10 $5y^2 + 70y + 245$

Exercise 6.5

1 $x = -\frac{2}{3}$

2 $x = 6$

3 $x = -3\frac{1}{2}$

4 $y = -43$

5 $x = \frac{2}{5}$

6 $x = -1\frac{1}{7}$

7 $x = \frac{1}{11}$

8 $x = \frac{3}{5}$

9 $x = +4 \text{ or} - 4$

10 $x = +9 \text{ or} - 9$

Exercise 6.6

1 $2(4x + 3y)$

2 $3(3y + 4z)$

3 $5(2x + y)$

4 $4(a + 4b)$

5 $5(2x + 3y)$

6 $9(x - 3y)$

7 $27(x - 3y)$

8 $5(6a - 5b)$

9 $3x(2x - 5)$

10 $7m(m - 7)$

Exercise 6.7

1 $(x + y)(x - y)$

2 $(t + y)(t - y)$

3 $(a + b)(a - b)$

4 $(a + 1)(a - 1)$

5 $(3g + h)(3g - h)$

6 $(4x + y)(4x - y)$

7 $(x + \frac{1}{2})(x - \frac{1}{2})$

8 $(3a + 4b)(3a - 4b)$

9 $(3y - z)(3y + z)$

10 $(4a + \frac{3}{5}b)(4a - \frac{3}{5}b)$

Exercise 6.8

1 $(x + 5)(x + 4)$

2 $(x + 7)(x + 5)$

3 $(x + 5)(x + 12)$

4 $(x + 7)(x + 3)$

5 $(x + 15)(x + 1)$

6 $(x + 3)(x + 5)$

7 $(x + 9)(x + 2)$

8 $(x + 11)(x + 1)$

9 $(x + 6)(x + 2)$

10 $(x + 9)(x + 5)$

Exercise 6.9

1 $(x + 1)(x - 2)$

2 $(x - 4)(x + 3)$

3 $(x + 5)(x - 3)$

4 $(x + 4)(x + 3)$

5 $(x + 7)(x - 2)$

6 $(x + 7)(x - 5)$

7 $(x + 9)(x - 2)$

8 $(x + 4)(x - 4)$ (did you use the difference of squares?)

9 $(x + 12)(x - 1)$

10 $(x + 10)(x - 9)$

Exercise 6.10

1   $x = a + b - y$ 2 $x = \dfrac{k + l}{v}$

3   $x = hj - b$ 4 $x = \dfrac{n(b - v)}{y}$

5   $x = b - \dfrac{h - d}{n}$ 6 $x = \sqrt{\dfrac{g^2 + k}{d}}$

7   $x = \dfrac{y}{f} - a$ 8 $x = \dfrac{ha}{m} - d$

9   $x = \dfrac{1}{9}\left(\dfrac{y}{d} - a\right)$ 10 $x = \dfrac{c - y}{m}$

Tutorial: Progress questions

1   $x^2 + 7x + 10$ 2 $x^2 + 10x + 21$

3   $y^2 + 6y + 8$ 4 $x^2 + x - 20$

5   $2x^2 - 6x - 8$ 6 $15x^2 - x - 10$

7   $12d^2 - 41d + 35$ 8 $12f^2 - 26f - 16$

9   $7g^2 - 25g + 12$ 10 $x^2 + 14x + 49$

11   $f^2 + 6f + 9$ 12 $x^2 - 16x + 64$

13   $d^2 + 4d + 4$ 14 $\dfrac{x^3 y^4}{z^4}$

15   $3b$

Chapter 7

Exercise 7.1

1   $x = 3, y = 4$ 2 $x = 5, y = 3$

3   $x = 2, y = 1$ 4 $x = 7, y = 10$

5   $x = 1, y = 2$ 6 $a = 5, b = 10$

7   $a = 9, b = 3$ 8 $a = 1, b = 6$

9   $x = 3, y = 2$ 10 $m = 4, n = 7$

Exercise 7.2

1   $a = 7, b = 2$ 2 $a = 4, b = 2$

3   $m = 6, n = 5$ 4 $x = 2, y = 3$

5   $r = 6, s = 7$ 6 $x = 7, y = 4$

7   $a = 15, b = 5$ 8 $m = 2, n = 7$

9   $a = 12, b = 13$ 10 $x = 1, y = 2$

Exercise 7.3

1   8 and 4   2   7 and 9

3   4 and 5   4   4 and 6

5   water 25p,   6   adult 70p,
    chocolate bar 20p   child 30p

7   adult £20.40,   8   chair £80,
    child £9.00   stool £25

9   ice cream 50p   10   one phone £19.99

Tutorial: Progress questions

1   $x = 7, y = 2$ 2 $x = 5, y = 4$

3   $x = 3, y = 1$ 4 $x = 12, y = 5$

5   $x = 2, y = 1$ 6   7 and 2

7   15 and 12   8   5 and 12

9   10 and 3   10   adult 90p, child 45p

Chapter 8

Exercise 8.1

1

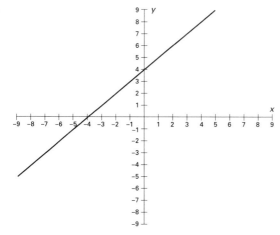

2

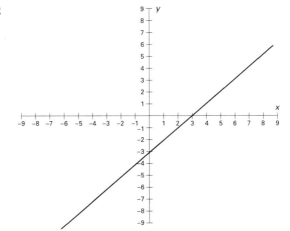

3

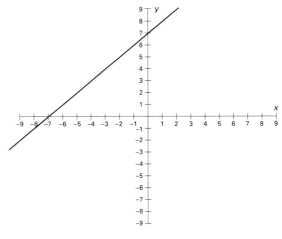

4

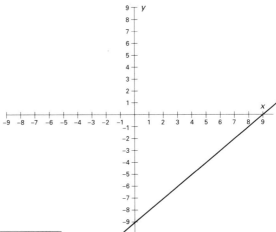

5

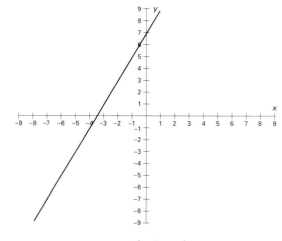

6

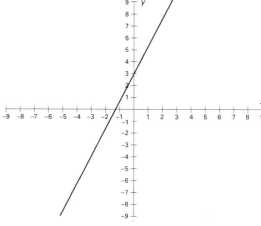

7

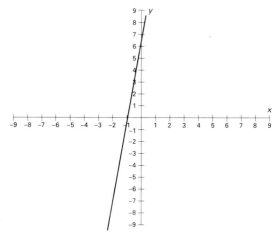

8

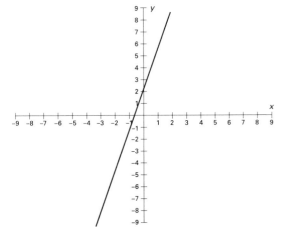

9

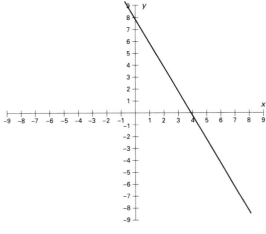

10

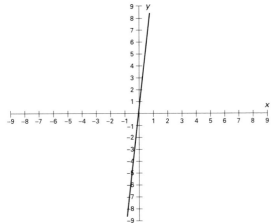

Exercise 8.2

1    $x = 5, y = 3$

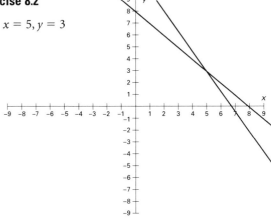

2    $x = 2, y = 1$

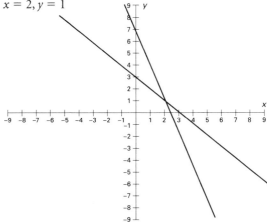

3    $x = 7, y = 10$

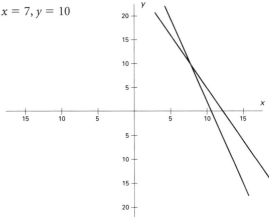

4 $a = 1, b = 2$

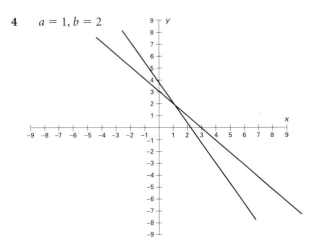

5 $m = 5, n = 10$

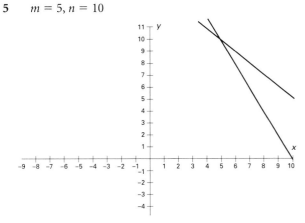

6 $x = 1, y = 4$

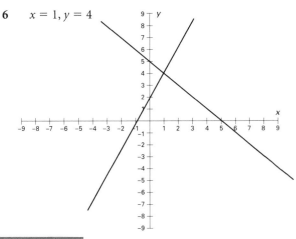

7    $z = 3, y = 2$

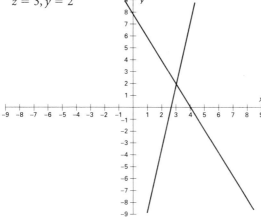

8    $x = 2, y = 22$

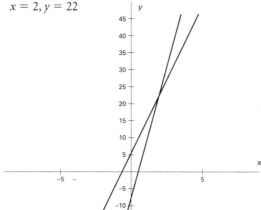

9    $a = 3, b = 4$

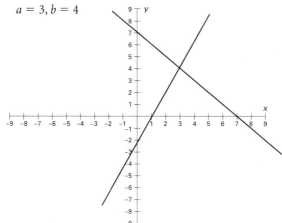

10 $x = 4.5, y = 5.5$

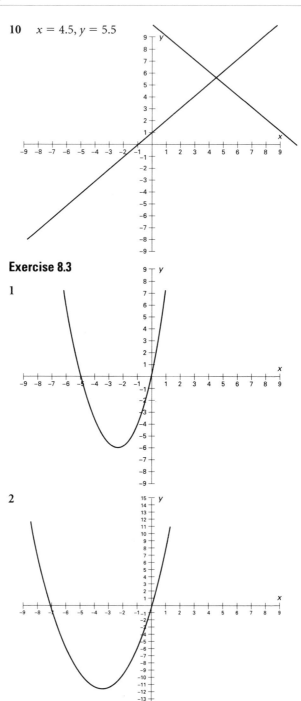

Exercise 8.3

1

2

3

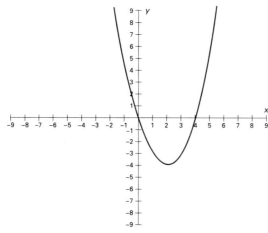

4

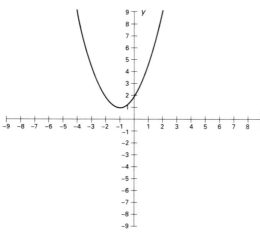

5

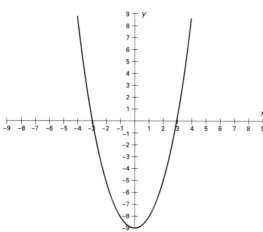

6

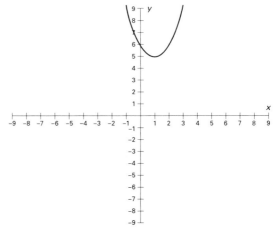

7

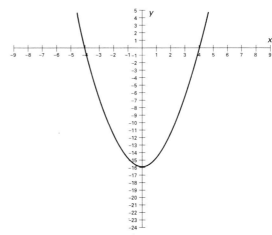

8

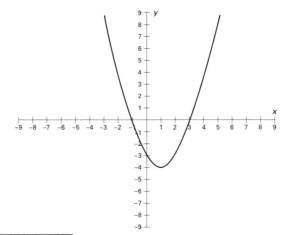

9

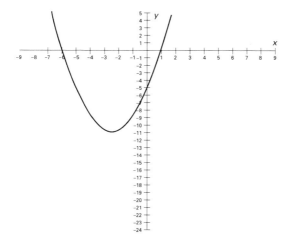

10

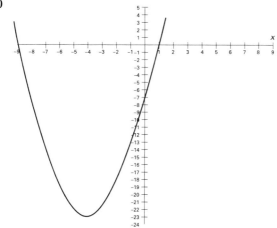

Chapter 9

Exercise 9.1

1	$(x + 6)(x + 2)$	**2**	$(x + 5)(x + 3)$
3	$(x + 10)(x + 2)$	**4**	$(x + 18)(x + 2)$
5	$(x + 5)(x + 7)$	**6**	$(y - 6)(y - 1)$
7	$(a + 1)(a - 12)$	**8**	$(b - 5)(b + 4)$
9	$(x - 6)(x + 4)$	**10**	$(y + 16)(y - 16)$

Exercise 9.2

1	$x = -10$ or -2	2	$x = -18$ or -2
3	$x = -7$ or -5	4	$y = +3$ or $+2$
5	$a = +3$ or $+4$	6	$b = +5$ or -4
7	$y = +3$ or $+3^*$	8	$a = +5$ or -1
9	$x = +10$ or -1	10	$b = -7$ or $+8$

* This answer is correct, it is known as a repeating root

Exercise 9.3

1	$x = 0$ or 4	2	$x = 0$ or -8
3	$x = 0$ or 3	4	$x = \pm 5$
5	$y = 0$ or 1.5	6	$x = \pm^1/_5$
7	$x = \pm 7$	8	$x = 0$ or $^1/_3$
9	$x = 0$ or -1	10	$y = 0$ or 1

Exercise 9.4

1	-0.438 or -4.561	2	-0.532 or -3.14
3	-0.293 or -1.707	4	0.192 or 3.475
5	1.358 or 0.442	6	-3.732 or -0.268
7	-1 or 1.667	8	0.377 or 7.956
9	-0.554 or 1.804	10	-0.483 or 1.150

Exercise 9.5

1	$(x + 3)^2 - 9$	2	$(x - 5)^2 - 25$
3	$(x + 1)^2 - 1$	4	$(x + 3)^2 - 8$
5	$(x - 3)^2 + 1$	6	$x = -6.464$ or 0.464
7	$x = -0.873$ or 6.873	8	$x = -2.414$ or 0.414
9	$x = -1.618$ or 0.618	10	$x = -0.618$ or 1.618

Tutorial: Progress questions

1	$(x + 6)(x + 2)$	2	$(x + 6)(x + 3)$
3	$(x + 12)(x + 2)$	4	$(x + 16)(x + 3)$
5	$x = -5.646$ or -0.354	6	$x = -2.175$ or -0.575
7	$x = -1$ or -0.5	8	$x = 0.2$ or 2
9	$x = 0$ or -6	10	$x = -0.449$ or 4.449
11	$x = -2$ or 0	12	$x = -5.828$ or -0.172

Chapter 10

Tutorial: Progress questions

1	3.343	2	-0.818

Index